Becoming Sexual

For Stephen Pfohl – an amazing professor and dear friend, whose wisdom and unfailing kindness always make all the difference.

Becoming Sexual

A Critical Appraisal of the Sexualization of Girls

R. DANIELLE EGAN

polity

First published in 2013 by Polity Press

Polity Press
65 Bridge Street
Cambridge CB2 1UR, UK

Polity Press
350 Main Street
Malden, MA 02148, USA

ISBN-13: 978-0-7456-5072-2
ISBN-13: 978-0-7456-5073-9(pb)

A catalogue record for this book is available from the British Library.

Typeset in 11 on 13 pt Monotype Bembo
by Servis Filmsetting Ltd, Stockport, Cheshire
Printed and bound in Great Britain by the MPG Printgroup, UK

The publisher has used its best endeavors to ensure that the URLs for external websites referred to in this book are correct and active at the time of going to press. However, the publisher has no responsibility for the websites and can make no guarantee that a site will remain live or that the content is or will remain appropriate.

Every effort has been made to trace all copyright holders, but if any have been inadvertently overlooked the publisher will be pleased to include any necessary credits in any subsequent reprint or edition.

For further information on Polity, visit our website: www.politybooks.com

Contents

Acknowledgments

Over the past three years, I have sought out numerous conversation partners and devil's advocates while working through an idea or line of reasoning. Most often, the conversation starts with the confused plea, "I am trying to get my head around this, do you have a minute?" Nine times out of ten, the person on the other line (phone or email) has said, "Absolutely;" they have given their time generously and pushed my thinking farther. Clearly, I am a very privileged woman. Feona Attwood, Lani Brunson, John Collins, Erin McCarthy, Stephen Pfohl, Liz Regosin, Emma Renold, Jessica Ringrose, Allen Shelton, Natalia Singer, Mary Jane Smith, Clarissa Smith, and Eve Stoddard have been particularly generous. Conversations with Barbara Baird, Sue Jackson, Keri Lerum, Susie Orbach, Juliet Schor, and Lisbet van Zoonen are also much appreciated.

The many years of friendship and intellectual collaboration with Gail Hawkes indelibly mark this book and my life in ways untold. Quite simply, *Becoming Sexual* would not have been possible without the work Gail and I did for *Theorizing the Sexual Child*.

Writing is a solitary business. All too often it takes me away from the people I love on weekends, holidays, and breaks from teaching – a special thank you to my family and friends who have been nothing but patient, loving, and supportive.

This book came into being as I began my training as a psycho-analyst at the Boston Graduate School of Psychoanalysis (BGSP). Although there were numerous times when I thought writing a book at the beginning of my clinical training and in the midst of my teaching was ill advised, to say the least, I do believe that the book is all the richer for it. The generative space created in my seminars with Dr Siamek Movahedi, Dr Mara Wagner, Dr Lynn Perlman, Dr Jane Snyder, and Dr John Madonna deepened my thinking and feeling on this topic and many others. The razor-sharp mind and important questions posed by Dr Stephen Soldz have been incredibly illustrative and kept me going back to the data.

Mark McClelland's generous invitation to present at the University of Wollongong was pure pleasure. The provocative conversations that took place as a result were particularly helpful. Emma Renold's invitation to give a lecture at the University of Cardiff and to be a part of a larger conversation on sexualization with Gail Hawkes, Jessica Ringrose, Valerie Walkerdine, Debbie Epstein, Rosalind Gill, Feona Attwood, Sara Bragg, Meg Barker, Laura Harvey, Robert Duschinsky, and numerous others felt, and still feels, like winning the lottery. Rarely does the door of opportunity open twice, but the conference *Pornified? Complicating Debates about the Sexualization of Culture* organized by Jessica Ringrose, Emma Renold, Meg Barker, and Rosalind Gill was equally invaluable. It was, by far, one of the best conferences I have had the pleasure to attend. My thinking on class and sexualization was deepened by the excellent questions posed during my talk for the Boston College Sociology Department, a place near and dear to my heart. I have had the pleasure of working with a group of smart, curious, brave, innovative, funny, activist-oriented, and badass students in Gender and Sexuality Studies at St. Lawrence University – my scholarly journey is inextricably tied to the work we do in the classroom, and for that I feel very lucky.

Through it all I have had the pleasure of working with a smart, passionate, and incredibly detail-oriented research assistant,

Jonathan Stopyra. His calm in the face of increasingly complicated requests for various demographic studies from three countries and sources to be added to the bibliography was awe-inspiring. If there was an MVP award for research assistance, he would get one!

Working with Polity has been pure pleasure. The support, guidance, and gentle nudging from my editor, Jonathan Skerrett, has been invaluable and much appreciated. At various times when this project felt like it would never come together, Jonathan's emails always soothed, clarified, and motivated. This book has been a labor of love. The team at Polity always made it clear that it was in good hands. For that I am incredibly grateful.

Words fail to adequately describe how lucky I feel about having Stephen Papson in my life. A brilliant interlocutor who always asks compelling and challenging questions and a caring partner who takes on all household responsibilities when I am anchored to the computer; who could ask for anything more? Your intellect, kindness, and care continue to astound me after all these years; Steve you are truly one of a kind.

Introduction:
Sexualization as a Social Problem

Children and young people today are not only exposed to increasing amounts of hyper-sexualized images, they are also sold the idea that they have to look "sexy" and "hot." As such they are facing pressures that children in the past simply did not have to face. As children grow older, exposure to this imagery leads to body surveillance, or the constant monitoring of personal appearance. This monitoring can result in body dissatisfaction, a recognized risk factor for poor self-esteem, depression and eating disorders. Indeed, there is a significant amount of evidence that attests to the negative effects of sexualization on young people in terms of mental and physical health, attitudes and beliefs.

Linda Papadopoulos (2010), *Sexualization of Young People Review*: 35

If girls learn that sexualized behavior and appearance are approved of and rewarded by society and by the people (e.g., peers) whose opinions matter most to them, they are likely to internalize these standards, thus engaging in self-sexualization.

American Psychological Association (2007) *APA Task Force Report on the Sexualization of Girls*: 2

After reading the quotes above, one comes away with a clear and unequivocal warning: sexualization is a ubiquitous force infecting the lives of girls. Sexualization, according to the American Psychological Association (APA) Task Force, results when any of the following four conditions have been met:

> a person's value comes only from his or her sexual appeal or behavior, to the exclusion of other characteristics; a person is held to a standard that equates physical attractiveness (narrowly defined) with being sexy; a person is sexually objectified – that is, made into a thing for others' sexual use, rather than seen as a person with the capacity for independent action and decision making; and/or sexuality is inappropriately imposed upon a person (APA 2007: 1).

In discussions of the sexualization of girls, it is the fourth condition, "sexuality is inappropriately imposed upon a person," that is most often cited. At first glance, this definition resonates with certain longstanding and influential feminist and left-leaning critiques of media and popular culture (Buckingham 2000, 2008; Gill 2007; Attwood 2009; Gonick et al. 2009; Duits and van Zoonen 2011); however, proclamations on the state of this condition rarely focus on media analysis. Indeed most often authors and activists turn their attention to individual outcomes of the effects of consumption in lieu of an analysis of cultural production. Warnings issue on the manifestation of sexualization signal a departure from feminist media criticism which focuses on issues of representation or cultural interrogations of an increasingly insidious capitalist formation toward the pathologization of practices, comportment, and clothing choice of girls who have been deemed to be sexualized (Duits and van Zoonen 2011).

Sexualization is said to defile innocence, leaving in its wake a promiscuous, emotionally deficient, and culturally bankrupt tweenager (Papadopoulos 2010). The toxic mix of sexualizing media and commodities (e.g., Bratz dolls, thongs, tee-shirts) transforms girls between the ages of 8 and 12 (or "tweens") into self-sexualizing subjects at risk for a host of mental, physical, cognitive, and relational problems. Reviewing such prognoses, one should not be surprised that sexualization narratives function in a deeply provocative manner – the combination of sexual corruption, defiled innocence, and its vision of an imperiled future – and often inspire strong visceral reactions. Really, how could it not? Popular rhetoric on sexualization relies upon and reproduces this potent affective brew to signal alarm bells and foment social action. While this rhetorical form often proves effective, its deployment of affect obscures the dubious epistemological, historical, and empirical foundations upon which its call to action rests.

Becoming Sexual is an attempt to render visible these assumptions and analyze their implications. Specifically, it examines the epistemological, historical, and affective work of this discourse[1] in order to analyze its social and political implications. Exploring how authors and activists draw on affect as well as longstanding ideologies of race, class, gender, age, and sexuality illuminates how sexualization is made meaningful and intelligible in public discourse. Shedding light on the phenomenological work of this discourse opens the critical space needed to raise larger social-psychoanalytic questions about what this type of thinking about children does for our culture and why we are so seemingly attached to it.

Sexualization as a Social Issue

Since 2006, a steady stream of policy papers, news stories, think-tank reports, parenting manuals, and opinion editorials chronicling the dangers of sexualization have appeared in the Anglophone West.[2] The British, Scottish, and Australian governments have commissioned reports and held hearings, and in 2010 the House of Representatives in the United States proposed a bill entitled the *Healthy Media for Youth Act*. Unlike other socially divisive topics (e.g., abortion, gay marriage, sex education), sexualization is an issue where politicians from the left and right are able to cross the aisle to find common ground. Although it would be erroneous to say that these responses share the same conception of the problem or offer uniform solutions, it is clear that sexualization has proved to be a particularly potent topic in political rhetoric in the Anglophone West over the past several years.

The Australia Institute and the American Psychological Association (APA) released reports within 12 months of one another on the topic which helped move sexualization, as a social problem, into the spotlight (Rush and La Nauze 2006a, 2006b; APA 2007). The Australia Institute's two reports, *Corporate Paedophilia* and *Letting Children be Children*, gained much media attention, spurred political action and were used during a hearing in the Australian Parliament, but their findings did not garner much coverage outside of Australia (Rush and La Nauze 2006a, 2006b). Conversely, the APA's *Task Force Report on the Sexualization of Girls* has become doctrinal in discussions of sexualization, and its findings are often taken for granted as fact in popular and academic circles both within and outside of the US (APA 2007). Numerous parenting guides and popular texts have also emerged from across the Anglophone West with titles such as: *The Lolita Effect: The Media Sexualization of Girls and What we Can Do About it* (Durham 2008); *Toxic Childhood: How the Modern World Is Damaging Our Children and What We Can Do about It* (Palmer 2007); *So Sexy So Soon: The New Sexualized Childhood, and What Parents Can Do to Protect Their Kids* (Levin and Kilbourne 2008); *Girls Gone Skank: The Sexualization of Girls in American Culture* (Oppliger 2008); *Living Dolls: the Return of Sexism* (Walter 2010); *What's Happening to Our Girls? Too Much, Too Soon: How Our Kids are Over Stimulated, Oversold and Oversexed* (Hamilton 2009b), and *Where has My Little Girl Gone?* (Carey 2011), as well as anthologies such as *The Sexualization of Childhood* (Olfman 2009) and *Getting Real: Challenging the Sexualization of Girls* (Reist 2009b). The combination of girls, sexuality, and pathological outcomes grabs our attention, insuring both its newsworthiness and the need for action. A search on LexisNexis revealed that since 2000 there have been 1,169 stories on the sexualization of children published in newspapers in Australia, the United States, and the United Kingdom. Sexualization has been featured in an untold number of blog entries, YouTube videos, television shows, radio programs, parenting newsletters, and workshops across the Anglophone West.

The central premise in much of the popular literature is that consuming sexualizing materials produces sexualized actions. Accordingly, consumption functions in a hypodermic fashion, whereby sexualized ideologies are injected wholesale into tween-aged victims. Sexualizing messages catalyze unsavory behavior, desire, and subjectivity (Egan and Hawkes 2007, 2009; Duits and van Zoonen 2011). As a result, girls "focus on sexualising themselves rather than pursuing other more age-appropriate activities," a choice which places their "gender identity, sexual attitudes, values and . . . capacity for love and connection" at risk (Rush and La Nauze 2006a: 3; Kilbourne, quoted in Tataro 2006). Other rampant psychopathological manifestations such as: binge drinking, eating disorders, lack of ability to bond or have strong relationships now and in the future, sextexting, and early pregnancy are also linked to consumption and self sexualization (Rush 2006, 2009; Rush and La Nauze 2006a, 2006b; APA 2007; Durham 2008; Farley 2009a, 2009b; Papadopoulos 2010). Within these texts, sexualized representations are conceptually equivalent with sexualized subjectivity and psychopathology. This raises a thorny issue: although we have seen an increase in sexualized commodities and representation in the Anglophone West, does this actually translate into promiscuity, pathology, and deficiency in tweenaged girls?

Placing the claims made in the sexualization literature against the vast terrain of quantitative and qualitative data gathered by scholars in public health, sociology, media studies, communication, psychology, history, and education reveals that all too often this discourse relies upon hyperbole instead of empirical research – something I discuss at length in chapter 1. In brief, what this research shows is that tweenaged girls are complicated subjects, neither asexual nor hypersexual. For example, girls are having less partnered sex than they did 20 years ago, are more responsible in terms of birth control when they do have vaginal/penile intercourse, and often have strong values and beliefs regarding sex and sexuality (CDC 2010; Fortenberry et al. 2010; Guttmacher Institute 2011). These data do not mean that media is inert or meaningless. A girl's relationship to media and popular culture is often complex, contradictory, and rarely straightforward (Mitchell and Reid-Walsh 2005; Celeste Kearney 2006, 2011). What it does highlight is that a girl's sense of self and sexuality should not be reduced to sexualization or any other monolithic effect.[3]

The schism between the empirical and rhetorical within the sexualization literature raises critical questions: Why are such hyperbolic claims so culturally palatable? Why do these ideas get reproduced with such ease? If our relations with girls reveal what ample data also back up – that, simply put, girls are complicated and diverse beings – then why is our culture so drawn to a vision of girls gone wrong? Are anti-sexualization authors being deceptive and/or manipulative? Anyone reading the popular literature on the topic can clearly see that authors and activists care deeply about the future of girls. Making sense of our cultural affinity for the sexually endangered as well as sexualized and sexualizing girl child is no easy task. Nevertheless, unraveling the phenomenological and affective work of this discourse helps reveal why the dangers associated with sexualization *seem to feel so real* for so many.

Cautionary narratives on the sexual corruption of children are firmly rooted in the Anglophone cultural imaginary, as are the epistemological claims and rhetorical form which support them. Tracing these cultural and historical foundation(s) upon which such claims are built illuminates the unacknowledged and long-standing preoccupations that help make the topic of sexualization meaningful or intelligible. Situating the discourse on sexualization within this context renders transparent its paradoxical nature and shifts analysis toward more complicated social-psychoanalytic queries. To state that the sexualization literature is misguided in its thinking about the nature of girlhood and consumption is limited because it misses the heart of the matter. The popular movement on sexualization speaks to a particular need in the Anglophone West, one that has a long history. The crux of the argument made throughout this book is that much of the popular rhetoric on sexualization is not really about girls in the messy and material sense, but rather that sexualization – as an outcome of increasingly insidious forms of patriarchal capitalism and popular culture – is actually an unacknowledged substitute for much more dire and disconcerting matters.

Conducting a rigorous textual analysis of the various material produced about sexualization in Australia, Britain and the United States illustrates that affective and ideological supposition often override complex empirical findings. This, coupled with the narrow framing of who is endangered – white, heterosexual, and middle-class girls – further highlights how the girl within sexualization is ultimately more metaphorical than material. It also helps bring to light critical questions about the function or use of this narrative within our cultural imaginary. It is my supposition that the discourse on sexualization is ultimately a cultural defense mechanism. Underneath the hyperbole lies the desire to defend against the unbearable costs of living in an increasingly fragmented, alienating, and unequal cultural landscape. As others have noted, economic despair and futility often spark populist responses, wherein impotence gets displaced into xenophobia, racism, and other forms of discrimination and violence (Bourke 2007; Asma 2009). Within this discourse, the costs of modern life get displaced into anxiety regarding the endless circulation of products (e.g., thongs, magazines, and dolls), people (pedophiles, celebrities, and bad influences), and conditions (sexualized media and increasingly loose sexual mores), which transform middle-class white girlhood into something monstrous and pathological.

In his writing on the philosophy of monsters, Stephen Asma notes that the word "monster" comes from the Latin root *monere*, "to warn" (Asma 2009). "To be a monster is to be an omen" or portent of impending doom (Asma 2009: 13). Whether it is the result of moral turpitude or fears regarding cultural and ideological shift within a society, the monster symbolizes a future in ruin. When reading descriptions of oral sex for pay and hyper promiscuity as well as psychopathological conditions such as depression or compassion deficit disorder, it soon becomes clear that within the popular literature the sexualized girl is a monster – the end point of defiled middle-class heterosexual femininity; and for more conservative authors, she also represents the erosion of the traditional family. A legacy of deeply problematic assumptions regarding race, class, gender, and sexuality informs this construction. The sexualized girl is a sign. She is emblematic of a fractured and corrupted middle-class status as well as an expression of nostalgia for times past when taste, status, age, difference, and control were believed to be more transparent and manageable. This is not to say that the child is never endangered or that capitalism is inert, but rather that the child in the fleshy sense is replaced by the girl, a figure, into which middle-class advocates project the vagaries of postmodern capital and its resultant social insecurity.

Repetition Compulsion and Historical Lineage

Psychoanalytic insights on repetition compulsion are particularly helpful when thinking about the obstinacy of such ideas and their currency in our cultural imaginary. At base, repetition compulsion functions as an unconscious pattern of behavior that resuscitates an unresolved trauma or conflict in various guises throughout an individual's life (Bibring 1943). Within this context, a person gets stuck in an often bewildering cycle as different protagonists rotate in as replacements destined to play out a familiar, and often unconsciously desired, script. Although these situations are painful, even traumatic, we tend to grow attached to their familiarity and seek out their presence.[4] It is important to note that patterns are not necessarily a carbon copy of the original; more often than not, they represent the defense mechanisms used to avoid the pain, confusion, rage, desire, and anxiety that would be evoked if one came into direct contact with the initial conflict or trauma. The replacement then is always already a derivative from the original, which makes its appearance all the more seductive while at the same time allowing it to retain its affective charge. As Freud noted in his earliest writings with Breuer, repression does not make trauma disappear, it only makes it harder to recognize due to its disguised form (Freud and Breuer 1895). Similarly, repetition compulsion does not eradicate the conflict; it only lessens its tension by prolonging it in a less traumatic form by proxy.

We need the threat of immanent sexual corruption, because it deflects the unbearable truth of what it means to live in a culture with decreasing social safety nets, joblessness, eroding security for the middle class, environmental degradation, increasing isolation and insecurity, as well as a shrinking public sphere through which to voice our concerns. By displacing our impotence onto something more manageable and potent – the cultural and sexual corruption of the girl child – our rage, disgust, and anxiety can be voiced and a fantasy of the future free of such defilement can be sought. The girl is a derivative – repellent in her sexualized form and freed from society in her innocence. This process is reproduced with ease because the child, as a cultural construct in the Anglophone West, functions as an endlessly permeable, but ultimately empty, receptacle into which adults can project our ills, anxieties, and aspirations (Walkerdine 1991, 1998; Kincaid 1998; Lamb 2001; Edelman 2004; Gonick et al. 2009; Stockton 2009).

As Karen Sternheimer has illustrated, our culture is besotted by sensational acts of sex and violence, directed toward or committed by the child, rather than the more mundane but far more pressing risks posed by poverty, neglect, and lack of medical care (Sternheimer 2006; see also Levine 2002). These cultural tendencies are not neutral; they inform policy, categories of normality and abnormality, and directly impact the lives of girls. The palliative effect of this cultural defense comes with a cost, the splitting of the girl child into one that is innocent and must be protected and the other who is viewed as sexually corrupting and reviled. Chapters 3 and 4 analyze the nature of this splitting to illuminate how loathing and disgust toward girls function as part of the affective undercurrent in the discourse on sexualization. For all the reasons stated above, an examination of the historical, epistemological, and affective architecture upon which such adult preoccupations and projections are built and made meaningful is a particularly important sociological and feminist endeavor.

Situating sexualization within a larger socio-historical context helps illuminate the continuities and discontinuities it shares with previous sexual protection movements in the Anglophone West (Egan and Hawkes 2010). My research with Gail Hawkes shows that since the mid 1800s the child's sexuality has been a key focal point for such movements (Egan and Hawkes 2010). Using Michel Foucault's analysis of the intersection of sexuality and biopower[5] as a starting point, we found that the child and its sexuality were foundational to the rise and validation of particular disciplines such as pediatrics, developmental psychology, hygiene, psychoanalysis, and sexology in the modern period. The production of expertise and moral authority often reflected larger conflicts of who "owned the child and its sex" as a site of knowledge – at various times medics, psychologists, pedagogues, psychoanalysts, sexologists, and feminist advocates all claimed the higher ground in these discursive struggles (Egan and Hawkes 2010). The espoused dangers to the child's sex were also, more often than not, allegories for larger societal ills (immigration, urbanization, racial purity) (Egan and Hawkes 2010). Although the discourse on sexualization draws on different conceptions of causation (e.g., the Internet, celebrity culture, and thongs) and outcome (hyper promiscuity), the manner in which the sexual child is conceptualized is strikingly consistent (Egan and Hawkes 2007, 2008, 2010). The following themes are part of a common conceptual architecture that has been taken for granted as natural by both anti-sexualization activists and their predecessors in times past.

Presence and Absence

The sexuality of the child is simultaneously present and absent within discourses on childhood sexuality. Although the child is conceptualized as having the physiological potential for sexuality (in the sense that they have reproductive organs and genitalia), this capacity should, under normal circumstances, be biologically, subjectively, and affectively absent until puberty (Foucault 1980; Egan and Hawkes 2010). In *The Choice: A Purity Booklet for Young Men* published in 1903, Australian purity advocate and politician, Richard Arthur, underscores this paradoxical conception when he cautions, "the boy knows nothing of this instinct, which is well; and I believe that most lads would not be disturbed by the vague stirrings of the sex sense, were it not that in many of them it is precociously developed by a constant turning of the attention to sex matters" (Arthur 1903: 4). Purity advocates believed one could direct the child's sexual instinct through moral education and in so doing protect them from perverse influences, compulsive masturbation, and a future life of debauchery (Egan and Hawkes 2007, 2010). Maggie Hamilton forwards a similar sentiment in her essay, "The seduction of girls: The human cost," published in 2009. Sexualizing media and commodities transform innocence into promiscuity and promote dangerous behaviors which threaten girls and society at large (Hamilton 2009a). Innocence within this framing is inherently asexual, and childhood is marked temporally by its innocence; in this sense childhood as a cultural category is intertwined with a particular conception of sexual dormancy (Egan and Hawkes 2010; Faulkner 2010). To rip away the veil of innocence, then, is to rob children of "a childhood" and instantiate eroticism. This is why eradicating corrupt influences is paramount within the literature.

Contemporary Dangers

Within protection narratives, risks normally fall into one of three categories: consuming sexually salacious materials (e.g., novels, comic books, rock music, television, magazines, and clothing items), playing outside the watchful gaze of parents (e.g., school yards, urban back alleys, or cyberspace), or interacting with "deviant" and/or socially marginal individuals (e.g., immigrants, homosexuals, sex workers, pedophiles, and knowing companions). The menacing nature of these influences is further exaggerated because they are deemed to be the result of threatening changes (urbanization, the Internet, the rise of social networking, the easing of censorship standards) that are unprecedented in their risk and impact (Egan and Hawkes 2010). Each generation is said to be facing and doing something their parents did not, and it is the immanence of peril which often legitimates calls for social and political action. Whether it is the comic book or the pedophile lurking behind every bush, the ignition of sexuality gets projected outward onto something or someone that must be censored or controlled.

British sexual hygienist, Walter Gallichan, provides a particularly illustrative example of this type of thinking when cautioning his readers to be wary of the danger posed by "inverts (homosexuals)," "prostitutes," "foul minded adolescents," and "bad parents," all of whom could render vulgar the sexual instincts of the child (Gallichan 1921: 12). Gallichan claimed that a single conversation could "blight" the future of the uninformed by initiating sexual thoughts, promiscuous sex, and resultant disease (Gallichan 1921). Echoing this sentiment some 86 years later, American feminist, Jean Kilbourne, warns, "our kids are growing up in a toxic cultural environment and it's awfully difficult for parents to stem the tide. We can tell parents, 'Don't let your kids dress this way,' but it's like saying the air is poisoned, don't let your kids breathe" (Kilbourne in Cabrera 2007).

Ignition incites Compulsion

Another common supposition at work in protection narratives is that, once stimulated, the child's sexuality becomes compulsive, dangerous, and uncontrollable (Hawkes and Egan 2008; Egan and Hawkes 2010). Because eroticism is catalyzed by salacious sources, it makes sense that the outcome would be deviant; however, the end point identified in many publications is hyper-compulsive and almost preternatural in its expression. In 1881 American pediatrician, William Humboldt Parker, argued that, once stimulated, "little female infants of tender years [produce] lascivious emotions by giving themselves up to furious masturbation" (Parker 1881: 77–8). Addiction to this solitary vice was said to lead to depravity, insanity, and possibly even death (Egan and Hawkes 2010). A cautionary tale written by feminist professor, Renata Klein, some 128 years later is eerily similar (Klein 2009: 133). The story revolves around a protagonist called Emma. Hoping to find her first boyfriend, Emma seeks guidance from numerous tween magazines. After reading the beauty advice found therein, Emma becomes bulimic and, once in a relationship, is "keen on having three Gardasil injections so she won't get cervical cancer from sex" (Klein 2009). Instead of the peace of mind promised in advertisements for the vaccine, she develops "a body rash" from the prescription. Confusing vaccination and birth control, Emma has unprotected sex with her boyfriend and ends up pregnant, dumped, and covered with "blisters." Although she tries to hide her mistakes by seeking an abortion, her sexual activities come to light, and she becomes the butt of jokes and ridicule, both in person and online. Once a star pupil, Emma's grades plummet along with her social status. Not surprisingly, depression sets in and she must start taking "SSRI antidepressants" in order to cope, but cannot help but feel that "she is a total failure" (Klein 2009: 133). Unlike the protagonists in treatises on masturbation phobia, Emma gets to live; however, it would not be beyond the bounds to say that Klein's narrative is one of social death. These descriptions of sexual corruption share an understated *schadenfreude-esque* quality; once lost, she is incapable of redemption and undeserving of empathy. The sexualized child must be destroyed mentally, emotionally, and physically. Once robbed of innocence, they are damaged goods.

The Need for Expertise

As I have noted already, anti-sexualization advocates argue that sexualization begets both sexual behavior and a host of dangerous mental health effects encompassing everything from "contagious acts of self harm" and crippling depression to thoughts of suicide (Rush 2006, 2009; Durham 2008; Levin and Kilbourne 2008; Oppliger 2008; M. Hamilton 2009a, 2009b; Travis 2010). We are also informed that sexualizing materials act as the "wallpaper" of a girl's life (Bailey 2011). Given the fragile and highly permeable nature of a girl's sexuality and the ubiquity of causative agents, one must wonder, how can sexualization be anything but a *fait accompli*? Nevertheless, anti-sexualization advocates, like their historical predecessors, insist that expert advice can offer parents preventative measures to stem the tide of risk.

Claims of expertise within protection narratives are grounded within a particular domain of knowledge (religion, medicine, psychology, or feminism) which is used to justify adult entry into this controversial and highly sensitive topic (Egan and Hawkes 2010). The presumption at work in these discourses is often one of parental ineptitude; in early writings, parents were seen as incapable of providing correct information, and poor parents, in particular, were believed to perpetuate harm (Walkerdine 1991, 1998; Walkerdine et al. 2001; Furedi 2002; Cross 2004; Egan and Hawkes 2010). In the current concerns, parents are framed as confused and befuddled, and in some texts, to blame for letting their children buy sexualizing products or engaging in "fat talk" (APA 2007; Egan and Hawkes 2008; Bragg 2012). A striking example from the past is provided in a speech given to the New York City School Board in 1916 by Maurice Bigelow within which he argued that professionals, not parents, should instruct children in sexual hygiene because, "most parents lack the skill and knowledge to impart adequate and accurate information on sex subjects to their children" (Bigelow 1916: A2). American Thomas Balliet's counsel to educators was equally strident; because parents promoted misinformation, it produced "a wholly wrong attitude toward sex" and as a result "tempt[ed] them to go wrong" (Balliet 1928: 4). It was for this reason, that even the *"most stupid teacher* [trained in the science of sex hygiene] *in school could not make blunders in giving this instruction comparable in their injurious effects to the teachings in the street to which all children are exposed"* (Balliet 1928: 4, emphasis in the original).

Authors writing on sexualization have come from various fields (communication, education, and psychology), nonetheless a psychological discourse is used to legitimate their claims. Although the *APA Task Force Report* has faced both conceptual and methodological criticism, it is circulated in an almost doctrinal manner in the literature (Egan and Hawkes 2008, 2012; Lerum and Dworkin 2009; Lumby and Albury 2011). However, it is also important to note that the popular literature on sexualization often constructs the problem in a manner that extends far beyond the claims made within the APA report. Nevertheless, a circularity exists within the sexualization literature; a psychological discourse and its production of a pathologized sexualized subject legitimates the protection movement (or field of expertise), which necessitates the creation of more advice which draws on a psychological frame, which recreates the pathologized sexualized subject. What gets ignored is a conception of girls as complex sexual citizens capable of engaging with media in ways that are both critical of, and complicit with, the ideologies of gender and sexuality forwarded in popular culture (Harris 2003; Celeste Kearney 2006, 2011; Jackson 2011; Phoenix 2011). As I will show in chapter 1, feminist psychology which challenges dominant conceptions of sexualization is also absent from the literature.

Think of the Children!

Historically, protection movements have inspired particularly problematic social practices such as circumcision to prevent masturbation, the creation of medical and psychological labels to stigmatize the expression of sexuality or desire, and the policing of marginalized populations (gays and lesbians, sex workers) under the guise of protecting children from sex (Angelides 2004, 2008; de Coninck-Smith 2008; Romesberg 2008; Schneider 2008; Egan and Hawkes 2010). It is my contention that the contemporary discourse on sexualization deploys many of the same epistemological assumptions and, as a result, suffers from the same problematic implications.

Nevertheless, it is critical to note that current concerns are gendered in a manner that is strikingly different from the ones raised in the late nineteenth and early twentieth centuries. Unlike the discourses of the past which focused on the perils of the child and sexuality, the current discourse on sexualization has narrowed its range of concern, to the distortion of a particular formation – the white, middle-class, and heterosexual tweenaged girl (Egan and Hawkes 2007, 2008, 2010; Renold and Ringrose 2008, 2011;

Robinson and Davies 2008; Lerum and Dworkin 2009; Lumby and Albury 2010; Smith 2010; Duschinsky 2011; Jackson and Vares 2011; Bragg 2012). The complex lives of girls get lost when translated into the sexualized girl. Deconstructing the implications of this shift is the focus of chapters 2 and 3.

In the art world, armatures are crucial, yet often unseen, structures made of mesh or wood that artists use to support the production of something larger – sculpture, three-dimensional models, puppets, etc. Drawing on the armature as a conceptual image, I analyze how the sexualized girl has been built upon a set of taken-for-granted and longstanding historical assumptions which give her form and affective life. Following the various lines of epistemological and historical support helps us understand why the deployment of the sexualized girl functions in a particular way and why she incites a particular affective response. After placing sexualization into a larger context, it becomes strikingly clear that, although there are clear distinctions in the construction of the child within the current discourse, our culture has formed a strong cathexis for and attachment to the sexual child and its double manifestation – as sexually defiled and sexually endangered. While the sexual child has had an important and recurring role in Anglophone culture since the early 1800s, it is equally true that children as sexual subjects or sexual citizens have been painfully absent (Irvine 1994, 2004; James et al. 1998; Renold and Ringrose 2008, 2011; Robinson and Davies 2008; Egan and Hawkes 2009, 2010; Duschinsky 2011; Jackson and Vares 2011; Bragg 2012; Robinson 2012).

Whether it be the risk to a child's sexual imagination via exposure to the novel, the comic book, the television, the record player, the music video, the magazine, the Internet, pornography, or the Bratz doll and the thong; or the hyper-promiscuous outcomes that result from consumption in the form of compulsive masturbation, necking and sex play, rainbow parties, or the ecstasy experienced in lap dancing on school buses and in games such as "assess my breasts," we clearly have a strong appetite for the sexual child (Walter, quoted in Hill 2010; Oppliger 2008; Kincaid 1992, 1998). We have grown attached to this repetition and find pleasure in our demands for protection as well as in our expressions of disgust, suspicion, and repulsion for the sexually corrupted. However, this pleasure must, in the end, be disavowed else our dominant cultural conceptions of the angelic child would come under suspicion (Kincaid 1998). It is for this reason that every new danger seems unique and unprecedented and every cautionary narrative is emptied of history. The questions that inform the rest of this book are: Why does this feel so compelling? How is it made meaningful? What does it do for us? And, to what end?

Unpacking the Discourse on Sexualization

Each chapter analyzes a particular set of epistemological, ideological, and historical assumptions that help make sexualization meaningful and emotionally compelling. Specifically, I highlight how four longstanding Anglophone anxieties get deployed in the discourse on sexualization: disquiet over unbounded female heterosexuality; the racialization of sexual innocence and anxieties regarding its defilement; middle-class fantasies and fears surrounding the eroticism of the working class; and finally, our culture's disgust, anxiety, and desire regarding the child's eroticism. It is important to understand that the ways in which we think about the girls and their sexuality is not "natural;" rather, it is shaped by the discourses and cultural narratives we produce about it. The manner in which sexualization is discussed – explicitly and implicitly – draws on longstanding historical preoccupations, fears, fascinations, desires, and discomforts, which fuel a particular conception of the problem; this framing grants some girls the hallow of innocence, normalcy, and health while others come to be viewed as promiscuous, deficient, and ripe for social sanction or therapeutic intervention. This is why a critical interrogation of the assumptions at work in this discourse is so pressing. *Becoming Sexual* is not about the sexual behavior of children and young people; rather, it is about the ways in which adults have constructed a particular social problem called sexualization.

Chapter 1 critically examines the logical and empirical claims underlying this discourse to render visible the paradoxical conception of causation and outcome at work in popular narratives on sexualization. Conducting an extensive review of the literature of materials from Australia, Britain, and the United States reveals how hyperbole and constructions of pathology often obscure far more pressing issues of representation. Chapter 2 deconstructs the manner in which gender, race, and sexuality are constructed within this discourse. One finds, in short measure, that the discourse on sexualization is not only gendered female, but that its primary focus is on the protection of a small subsection of girls – namely those who are white, heterosexual, and middle class. Exploring how longstanding anxieties surrounding femininity, the family, and whiteness underpin this discourse illuminates that the girl within sexualization narratives is more metaphorical than material. Chapter 3 offers an in-depth analysis of the ways in which taste, comportment, and class are deployed in sexualization narratives. Unpacking the manner in which the working class and its eroticism are conceptualized by middle-class advocates highlights how fears of class contagion are central to this discourse. Chapter 3 further illuminates how the disgust and anxiety surrounding the working class is actually a displacement for the increasingly fragile state of the middle class in our contemporary culture. Chapter 4 forwards a psychoanalytic reading of the implicit disgust and loathing at work in the discourse on sexualization. Drawing on the work of Melanie Klein, this chapter shows that more often than not innocence functions as a guilt formation rather than a starting point in the conception of the girl in popular narratives on the topic. The Conclusion explores how and why the deconstruction of affect is crucial for research on "social problems" and offers a starting point for how we might move forward in the future. Attending to the evocative quality of this discourse offers a framework for examining the affective, historical, ideological, and epistemological work of narratives on sexualization. It is my hope that my analysis will complicate reductionist thinking on the sexual child and add to the important conversations taking place on the sexual citizenship of children (Angelides 2008; Egan and Hawkes 2010; Ringrose 2013).

1

What is Sexualization?

It is a drip, drip effect. Look at porn stars, and look how an average girl now looks. It's seeped into everyday: fake breasts, fuck-me shoes . . . We are hypersexualising girls, telling them that their desirability relies on being desired. They want to please at any cost.

Papadopoulos, quoted in Travis (2010)

Introduction

The twining of defiled innocence, precocious sexual promiscuity with a clearly defined antagonist – popular culture – makes this discourse deeply seductive and its rhetoric self-evidently true. Its omnipresence and the consequences involved make critique almost impossible and often politically suspect – after all, who can be for the sexualization of young girls? Within this context the question, what is sexualization?, becomes all the more salient. Is it a social phenomenon, an event, a type of representation, or an individual condition? Is it all of the above and more? Amidst claims of girls being taken in by a life of "fake breasts," "fuck me shoes," and desires "to please at any cost," it is not hard to imagine why someone might experience powerful emotions when reading these warnings (Papadopoulos 2010; Harris 2010). This deployment of affect makes a more measured response far more challenging and the need for a critical exploration of the emotional work of anti-sexualization narratives all the more imperative. What happens when one moves beyond the affective in order to deconstruct the knowledge claims underlying this discourse? And, equally, what are the social and political implications of such assertions? The goal of this chapter is to wade through the term "sexualization" and the ways in which it is conceptualized in order to render visible the epistemological assumptions at work within contemporary writing on the issue. In so doing, this chapter will forward a number of questions and themes that will be explored in depth throughout the rest of the text.

Conceptualizing Sexualization

According to most authors on the topic, sexualization is pandemic in its reach and impact. Conceptualized as a dangerous influence that permeates the cultural landscape of girls' lives, sexualization "places all children at risk for internalizing impoverished models of gender and human relationships" (Olfman 2009: 1). As omnipresent as oxygen and as toxic as poison, it seems impossible to escape this phenomenon. Whether it is in the form of erotic media messages, overly sexy clothing, salacious costumes for Halloween (a holiday termed "Skankoween" in much of the literature), sexual advice being offered in tween magazines, or in the toys scattered across a girl's bedroom, advocates warn that "girls are [being] encouraged to act like teenagers just a few years after shedding their diapers" (Linn 2009: 49; see also Levin and Kilbourne 2008; Farley 2009a, 2009b; M. Hamilton 2009a, 2009b).

In large part, this phenomenon is seen as an outcome of a culture bent on enticing unwitting girls into becoming lifelong consumers and ultimately passive female subjects. Seducing them through sexy and provocative images akin to those featured in pornography is, according to radical anti-sexualization advocates, how this goal is achieved (Durham 2008; Levin and Kilbourne 2008; Reist 2009a; Dines 2011). Girls are "taking their [sexual] script directly from pornography" or what some activists in the Anglophone West have termed "pornification" – a cultural form so ubiquitous that women and girls find it near impossible to avoid (Papadopoulos, quoted in Travis 2010; see also Durham 2008; Farley 2009a, 2009b). In 2009, Jacqui Smith, the then Home Secretary to Gordon Brown's Labour government, expressed her concerns over these developments when she commented that sexy clothes, such as "Playboy T-shirts," pressure girls "to appear sexually available at an increasingly younger age" and may lead to a future of sexual violence (Smith, quoted in Travis 2009). Although the landscape of cultural representation is criticized, the psychological effects of sexualization are the primary cause for concern within much of the popular literature.

Authors state that sexualization creates a future of self-doubt, a lack of ability to form intimate relationships and fosters self-destructive impulses such as binge eating, sextexting, pregnancy, sex with older men, prostitution, and even suicide (Rush and La Nauze 2006a, 2006b; APA 2007; Durham 2008; Oppliger 2008; Farley 2009a, 2009b). Once lured, we are told that girls travel blindly down the road to ruin. Even though anti-sexualization rhetoric begins with a critique of media and popular culture, too often authors and activists turn their attention to individual outcomes in lieu of an analysis of cultural production. Although it might be tempting to view these distinctions as simple differences in what a methodologist might call the "unit of analysis" (e.g., focusing on the individual versus the culture industry) or a case of disciplinary distinctions (e.g., psychology versus sociology, cultural studies, or media studies), this logic becomes flimsy when one begins to map the epistemological and empirical assumptions at work in the literature. This chapter focuses primarily on claims surrounding the transformation of sexual subjectivity and resultant production of pathology in the narratives on sexualization.

Within the literature, sexualization operates in a tautological fashion. Pornographic-like advertisements, media, and objects produce the desire to purchase, which promotes a longing to look like and, even more disturbing for many, the impulse in girls to emulate the women in the pornographically inspired images that seduced them in the first place. This cycle is further exacerbated by exposure to more media and consumer objects. Consumption leads to unequivocal acceptance and, as a result, pathology. Reviewing these claims, it is no wonder that such a message would create anxiety, disgust, and anger in many readers, not to mention in most parents. The angst surrounding sexualization, however, is not confined to a particular subset of left-leaning criticism.

In his successful bid to become Britain's Prime Minister, Conservative Party leader David Cameron echoed concerns about sexualization, promising that, if elected, he would free the children of Britain from the deleterious influences of advertising and overly sexy toys and clothing. For Cameron, ridding the country of such materials would ensure that "our children get a childhood" (Cameron, quoted in BBC 2010). As Prime Minister, he commissioned Reg Bailey, head of the Mother's Union in Britain, to create a second report, *Letting Children be Children*, which was released in 2011 – less than a year after the Papadopoulos report, the *Sexualization of Young People*, written for the Labour government. Bailey's report shies away from a critique of patriarchy and was more careful in its use of causal language; nonetheless, it relied upon and reproduced a similar set of assumptions regarding sexual materials and childhood corruption (Bailey 2011; Curtis 2011; Barker and Duschinsky 2012). In a less official context, Kristen Fyfe, a commentator from the Culture and Media Institute, an organization dedicated to "preserve and help restore America's culture, character, traditional values, and morals against the assault of the liberal media elite" and to "promote [the] fair portrayal of social conservatives and religious believers in the media," expressed her anger over the social implications of sexualization (Fyfe 2008). Like her counterparts on the left, she is upset by the dearth of media coverage on this important issue. Instead of focusing on the real issue – "the culture of sex aimed at girls and talk about the racks and racks of low-cut tops and cut-down-to-*there* jeans that fill the malls across America" and the dangers of "sex-filled music lyrics found on iPods plugged into the ears of hundreds of thousands of kids," media stories are limited to salacious features covering "Skank-o-ween" costumes (Fyfe 2008).

Although critics bemoan the lack of coverage on sexualization, it is anything but a dead topic in the media. According to a LexisNexis search, the phrase "children + sexualization" has been featured in 935 newspapers since 2000. Searching the phrase "children + sexualisation" within the same time frame produces 234 results. The combination of sex, childhood, and popular culture creates a strong media response – and thus the theme of sexualization has had a prominent place in the news all over the Anglophone West. Ironically, media both perpetuates and foments the story of sexualization and is said to be one of its primary catalysts. Nevertheless, in an organization that might otherwise place feminist concerns under the umbrella of the "liberal elite" and a danger to traditional family values, movements of protection often require the strangest of bedfellows. Fyfe, for example, draws on the work of feminist educator Jean Kilbourne to support her critique of the media and overly sexual clothes. In particular she highlights their shared dismay over the growing disconnect between the advice offered in popular cultural media outlets and parental instruction. Levin and Kilbourne's *So Sexy So Soon: The New Sexualized Childhood, and What Parents Can Do to Protect their Kids* details how one of the effects of sexualizing media is to create "premature adolescent rebellion" in girls, thereby fomenting hostility between tweens and their parents (Levin and Kilbourne 2008: 25; see also Fyfe 2008).

Coalitions between the religious right and a particular subset of radical feminist activists have a long history in movements seeking sexual reform – particularly ones attempting to ban cultural materials and/or practices deemed morally and sexually corrupt (Luker 1998; Hunt 1999; Mort 2000; Egan and Hawkes 2010; Faulkner 2010). One need only look to the anti-obscenity campaigns of the Comstock era in the United States and the movements against prostitution in England, Australia, and the United States that took place at the turn of the century to gain a sense of their shared history in this common cause (Gorham 1982; Mort 2000; Brown 2002, 2004; Agustin 2007; Egan and Hawkes 2010).[1] During the 1970s and early 1980s, these groups formed strategic coalitions to

ban pornography and prostitution in much of the Anglophone
West (Rubin 1992; Egan 2006; Agustin 2007).[2]

Although the politico-moral impetus driving these groups
differs – moral depravity and sin versus patriarchal exploitation and
objectification, respectively – both imbue sexually salacious material with an unparalleled power of influence, one that is particularly
dangerous if found in the wrong hands. Whereas in the past, the
locus of concern was the risk posed to men, women, and children
by erotic or "perverse" materials – albeit in strikingly different
ways and toward different ends – the contemporary movement
on sexualization focuses on a singular source, the tween-aged girl
(the implications of which will be discussed at length in chapter 2).
She is conceptualized as highly vulnerable and deeply dangerous,
because once sexualized she readily embodies and enacts the ethos
of a pornified culture and "wants to please at any cost" (Farley
2009a, 2009b; Papadopoulos 2010; Dines 2011). In this sense, the
sexualized girl has come to replace another longstanding symbol
of cultural decay – the fallen woman. Like the prostitute of the
past who was conceptualized as both a victim of new urbanism
and male lust as well as a risk to respectable families, girlhood
innocence within the anti-sexualization literature is framed as both
endangered and unstable, and, once stimulated, a threat to individuals and society (Gorham 1982; Mort 2000; Brown 2002, 2004).

According to many anti-sexualization critics, sexuality should
be an "independent island nation" untainted by the avarice of
corporations and free of cultural influence (Peters 2002). As activ-
ist Cynthia Peters warns, when our culture begins to send the
message to very young children that we should "disassociate sex
from nonmarket feelings (pleasure, desire, intimacy) and associate
it instead with consumable superficial feelings, you'll not only keep
the rabble in line, you'll have them lined up at the mall" (Peters
2002). The impact of sexualization extends beyond the pressure to
dress in a particular way – it infiltrates the mental and imaginative
life of the child. Susan Linn argues that "an endless, intensifying
loop of commercially constructed fantasies" tarnishes a child's
imagination, limiting their vision of what is possible by defining
what their future should be" (Linn 2009: 40). Instead of wanting to

play hero or some other form of empowered play, girls get sucked into "media-driven scripts characterized by entitlement, helplessness and dependence" (Linn 2009: 33). Mary Beth Sammons, *Circle of Moms* contributor, argues that this is evidenced by the fact "Toys are growing up, shedding their baby fat, and waxing their legs. Even Disney fairies are boasting hourglass figures and trading in their innocent ballerina look for saucy wardrobes" (Sammons 2011). "Looking in mirrors, walking in fancy high heels and vamping," while playing "dress up" are illustrations of sexualized play that takes place in the classroom and the home (APA 2007: 16). Although dress-up may have had a strong place in the life histories of many adults (including the author of this book), this form of imaginative fun is different because of the corporate narratives children draw on, which are inspired by the scantily clad outfits of Bratz dolls and other culturally backward sources.

Sexualization is believed to infiltrate a child's innocence, which under normal circumstances is considered sacrosanct and inherently asexual, and it is for this reason that its results are so perilous and dangerous. Analyzing the increasing encroachment of consumer capital in the lives of children is deeply important sociologically and politically; however, the equation forwarded by Peters and Linn is ultimately problematic. The implicit assumption is that sexual innocence and, by implication, childhood is a state of nature which stands outside of culture and capitalism; while this is undoubtedly a potent and provocative stance, it ignores the implications of constructing the child and its sexuality in such a manner. This supposition strips away the socio-historical legacy of innocence, as a social construct, and how it has been used ideologically to support dubious social policies, bolster deeply problematic conceptions of race and nation, and as a weapon against poor families (Zelizer 1985; Sanchez-Eppler 2005; Anderson 2006; Cunningham 2006; Egan and Hawkes 2010; Faulkner 2010; Bernstein 2011). It also seems to turn a blind eye to the fact that innocence also sells and has its own market niche – Australian photographer Anne Geddes, for example, has created a veritable industry exploiting our sentimental attachment to innocence with her images of angelic babies as fairies, flowers, and animals on everything from dolls, calendars, mugs, and posters, to pregnancy diaries, baby books, and invitations. In addition, images of sexual innocence are used to sell clothing brands, baby food, and political candidates, to name only a few. More importantly, conflating childhood with innocence may unwittingly deem any child who consumes sexualizing products to be outside of childhood (because she is no longer innocent) and thus a byproduct of cultural contamination.

Comedian and cultural critic Celia Rivenbark highlights this in her essay on school shopping entitled, "Stop Dressing Your Six-Year-Old like a Skank" (Rivenbark 2006), in which she recalls a particularly traumatic trip to the mall where the only clothing choices available in the "awfulness that is tweenland" were "well, slutty looking" or "hooker" wear (Rivenbark 2006: 28). Although she will have to search high and low, she vows that her daughter will avoid all clothes touched "by the wand of the skank fairy" (Rivenbark 2006: 28–9). A similar lament is offered by Jennifer Moses in a recent *Wall Street Journal* editorial, "Why do we let them dress like that?" which details her attempt to make sense of why mothers buy their 12- and 13-year-old daughters clothes with "plunging necklines, built-in push-up bras, spangles, feathers, slits and peek-a-boos" (Moses 2011). Moses, like Rivenbark, forwards maternal responsibility as key to impeding the continuation of girls dressing and, by implication, acting like "prostitutes."

In more serious tomes, commentators warn that "popular culture markets prostitution to girls as glamorous, fun, sexy and an easy source of income" and normalizes participation in "games" like "assess my breasts" (Farley 2009b: 144; see also Walter, quoted in Hill 2010). Sexualization is conceptualized as boundless in its effects – it penetrates cultural production, the economy, and taints our most intimate subjective sensibilities (APA 2007; Durham 2008; Reist 2009a; Papadopoulos 2010). Operating as the lens through which parents, teachers, and peers come to evaluate the appearance and actions of girls, authors argue that sexualization shapes the standards by which girls are assessed in multiple domains (APA 2007; Levin and Kilbourne 2008; Hamilton 2009b; Reist 2009a). Parents are as culpable of sexualizing their children as corporations when they engage in "fat talk," purchase sexy commodities, and in the most extreme cases pay for plastic surgery (APA 2007; Farley 2009a, 2009b; Bailey 2011; Carey 2011). Girls find themselves in a socio-educational context that conflates erotic appeal with popularity (APA 2007: 17). "When sexual allure becomes girls' only pathway to power and self worth," Barbara Berg warns, "the roles of achievement, talent and being a decent person are diminished" (Berg 2009: 241). Parents, teachers, and peers may be unwittingly perpetuating a culture of disempowerment. Within this frame, girls are conceptualized as passive in the extreme, open receptacles into which sexualization messages are deposited and then enacted. The painful consequences of hegemonic beauty standards and restrictive gender stereotypes should not be discounted; rather, it is the assertion of uniform reception and pathology that should give us pause.

The question then becomes, to what effect? According to advocates, tawdry toys, pornified media, and salacious clothing are the ground from which the feminine and its eroticism get produced. Sexualizing materials eclipse and override every other cultural form. Despite the multiplicity of cultural representations, parental influence, school messages, or the various other ways in which a girl's eroticism is socially sanctioned by peer groups (e.g., slut bashing), the allure of sexualization is said to be more powerful.

From Objectification to Sexual Action

Sexualized behavior and its consequences unfold in the following manner: mimicry, internalization, and finally self-destructive impulses that impinge upon the present and shape the future. While "act[ing] out in sexually provocative ways" may at first be the result of modeling, the authors of the American Psychological Association Task Force on sexualization caution that it would be erroneous "to state that girls are freely choosing these behaviors" (APA 2007: 18–19). Australian feminist Renata Klein further illuminates the effects of sexualization when she states: "surrounded by so much grown-up stuff, many girls perform these roles [engaging in seductive looks and behavior] in real life" (Klein 2009: 131).

Media begets desire which begets action which then becomes compulsive; and "ready or not," we are told by conservative critic Kay Hymowitz, the outcome is shocking and deeply disturbing (Hymowitz 2000, 2002). Eagerly simulating "sexual intercourse" and "masturbation" on buses and spending lots of time "grabbing each other's buttocks and breasts" is just the tip of the iceberg (Hymowitz 2000: 164). The gravity of this outcome is further crystallized in the rhetorical question posed by Australian Emma Rush: "How do we then expect [girls] to behave if an older man approaches apparently offering romance?" (Rush 2006). Apparently after a consistent dose of sexualizing messages, the answer becomes an inevitable, "Yes, I am interested." What may begin with simple modeling often ends with a future in ruins. Sexualization produces pathological subjects. Inaction by adults within this discourse is *de facto* consent; we are told that we will only have ourselves to blame for bringing up a generation of girls whose primary aspirations are lap dancing and lip gloss if we sit idly by and do nothing (Hymowitz 2000, 2002; Klein 2009; Farley 2009a, 2009b; Papadopoulos 2010). Given the extreme nature of its potential effects, how exactly does this transmutation take place?

Sexualizing materials catalyze a girl's sexual emergence and in so doing foster a particular set of desires and activities. Three areas that were once pure become corrupted by the imprint of sexual-izing media: the "free island" of a girl's sexuality, her imagination, and finally her innocence – and thus, the essence of childhood itself. Because sexualization extends beyond the realm of sexual precocity into more systemic problems (in the physical, mental, and psychic realms), undoing its influence seems almost impos-sible (Rush and La Nauze 2006a, 2006b; APA 2007; C. Hamilton 2009). For example, exposure is said to produce a "minefield of mental health" issues, which in turn create a "cluster of symptoms" such as "self-loathing, depression, addiction, anxiety and difficulty being close" (Biddulph 2009: 164). Less likely to form caring rela-tionships now and in the future, tweens face a life of isolation and a lack of love (APA 2007). Narcissistically consumed with their looks, girls lose interest in other social and scholastic achievements and must deal with the effects of cognitive delay (Rush and La

Nauze 2006a; APA 2007; Berg 2009; Linn 2009). Adrift in this sea of cognitive, behavioral, and mental health issues, sexualized girls suffer a fate worse than Narcissus. Sexualization seems to trigger a change whereby once-innocent girls become self-involved, sexually salacious, cognitively delayed, and depressed (Biddulph 2009: 164). If not rescued, girls are subject to a damnable fate indeed.

Melissa Farley adds an even more disturbing prognosis to the already terrifying diagnosis of sexualization discussed thus far. "As girls are becoming increasingly sexualized by popular culture, they are more likely to be the object of men's sexual fantasies, and because children are more easily controlled than adults, they are a lucrative sector of the prostitution market" (Farley 2009b: 144). According to Farley, impersonating "smiling strippers and escorts" may be seen as a developmental milestone along the path to child prostitution or the lap dance couch (Farley 2009b: 151). How does this take place? After being cast as the object of desire in various media formats, the demand for girls increases. The desire for a future in the sex industry is inculcated by consumption; once sexualized, girls seem to travel almost lockstep toward this destination. Sex work is assumed to be the outcome of taint, and thus sex workers, as subjects, are corrupted. Poverty, familial conditions, curiosity, desire, abuse, addiction, economics, and a whole host of other complex factors seem to give way to the media and commodities as the primary causal factor for work in the sex industry.

We are warned that even when girls are not on the street being guided by a pimp, they are prone to organize and "enact the sex of prostitution" or engage in striptease (Farley 2009a: 120; see also Oppliger 2008). As Farley decries,

> casually fellating boys at parties is normative for girls, according to a recent Canadian article. One girl repeated the classic pimp's argument for prostitution, noting that if she was already fellating two or three boys every weekend at parties for free, she might as well do the same with five or six boys and get paid for it (Farley 2009a: 120).

Sexualization promotes a cascading effect that starts with Bratz or bralettes and ends with girls performing fellatio for pay in the suburbs as corrupt entrepreneurs or as child prostitutes under the sway of their pimp. The message sent to girls is painfully clear – sex equals danger, damage, work in the sex industry, and social sanction. The boundary between innocence and compulsion is exceedingly fragile, and once this line has been crossed, a girl becomes something else – someone beyond (or maybe not worth) intervention. In effect, sexual girls become the problem, not sexism.

As illustrated in the Introduction, this conception of cause and outcome has a long history in the Anglophone West. Such claims are also reminiscent of a panic started during a 2003 episode of *The Oprah Winfrey Show* entitled, "Is your child leading a double life?" Guest experts struck fear in the hearts of the primarily female audience with cautionary tales about a rash of "rainbow parties" taking place in the cities and suburbs all over the United States. After donning a signature hue of lip gloss, girls were to said to engage in what seemed to be an almost industrial line form of fellatio on boys – the end result being a rainbow of colors on the penises of participants who would then compare to see who had the most stripes. Notwithstanding the substantial outcry, news coverage, and subsequent novel, *Rainbow Party*, that were inspired by the goings-on at such events, rainbow parties were ultimately declared more urban legend than fact (Lewin 2005). One might imagine that the salacious quality of these types of claims might raise the specter of doubt regarding their credibility; nonetheless, the idea that a child's sexuality, once ignited, becomes almost preternatural in its compulsivity (e.g., rainbow parties share this logic with fears of children masturbating until death or insanity in the early 1800s) has had a prominent place in the Anglophone cultural imaginary (Egan and Hawkes 2010). Such assumptions and concomitant anxieties are often featured in shows dedicated to uncovering the "secret lives" of teens and tweens, such as the 2004 NBC/ *People* magazine collaboration featured on the popular American morning show, *Today*. The findings from this collaboration were advertised with the tagline, "Is oral sex the new goodnight kiss?" Interestingly, the "Secret lives of teens survey" found that only 10 percent of respondents between the ages of 13 and 16 had ever engaged in oral sex (Tauber et al. 2005). Although these findings were clearly known in advance, producers played upon this cultural preoccupation by going with this question instead of another, "Why do we think teens are hypersexual? What every parent should think about." One must wonder why such outlandish claims – that tween and teenage girls are enthusiastically engaging in group oral sex at parties and for pay, no less, because for them it's like the kissing booths of their grandmothers' generation – could be culturally credible and disseminated with such ease in the first place?

In *Fast Girls: Teenage Tribes and the Myth of the Slut*, Emily White argues that assertions such as the ones discussed above comprise the most common trope in the "slut stories" that circulate in high schools across the United States (White 2004). According to White, the slut, as a mythic figure, is as central to high-school culture as the cafeteria and the prom. In interviews with girls cast as the high-school slut and with those who perpetuated such rumors, White found that it was the "train job" rumor that solidified a girl's place as "the slut" of a particular high school (White 2004: 45). Joyfully performing fellatio on as many males whenever and wherever possible in a single night (the definition of a "train job"), the subject of the rumor is presumed to be voraciously sexual and completely indiscriminate and thus deserving of scorn and social sanction. Once deemed the protagonist, the girl becomes a social pariah and all too frequently subject to verbal, physical, and sexual harassment (White 2004). She marks the boundary of gendered and sexual acceptability as "a danger sign" and functions as cautionary tale (White 2004: 13). According to White, the slut, as a mythic figure, helps young people make sense of the tumultuous nature of their sexual becoming – however, it also comes with a painfully high cost for those stamped with this stigmatizing label (White 2004).

To be clear, I am not claiming, nor do I believe, that authors writing on sexualization are like the high-school rumor mongers interviewed by Emily White. Rather, I draw on White to raise questions about the nature and style of rhetoric employed within the sexualization literature in order to think critically about its implications. Although anti-sexualization advocates are thoroughly invested in trying to make the world a better place for girls, I wonder whether some of the rhetorical strategies employed in their discourse unwittingly serve the same purpose as the high-school slut story. Like the figure of the high-school slut, the sexualized girl is unbridled in her sexuality and seems to take pleasure in the sexual servicing of boys and men; moreover, she shows little interest in her own eroticism or pleasure. Among the authors I have read, there is no mention that sexualization fosters a compulsive search for orgasm in girls or even a concern for their own pleasure; rather, their pleasure is like their reception of sexualized messages – passive. Unlike high school, where one girl becomes the scapegoat in the collective drama of sexual becoming, in the sexualization literature a particular category of girls is endangered (white, middle-class, and heterosexual) and fears of promiscuity begin at a much younger age. Every white middle-class girl becomes a potential protagonist in the mythic fantasy of what happens when good girls go bad. Why are assumptions that skirt painfully close to something like slut shaming being perpetuated within a certain subset of feminist discourse? How do such assertions come to feel so natural? Do we need to destroy girls in order to save them? Why isn't a critique of representation enough? One answer may be that the construction of the girl child within these narratives speaks to a cultural phenomenon that extends far beyond the everyday lives of tweens.

The sexualized girl and her innocent counterpart are potent cultural constructions which symbolize a much larger and irresolvable set of cultural insecurities. Deconstructing their evocative nature requires mapping how longstanding Anglophone preoccupations and anxieties come together to make the figure of the girl endangered meaningful. Efforts to deny and control the sexuality of the child may reflect larger socio-cultural endeavors (ones which are almost impossible in our postmodern moment) to reaffirm and reinstantiate boundaries of gender, sexuality, race, class, and age. Before examining the implications of these desires in the chapters that follow, I will illuminate the logical suppositions underpinning this discourse and its use of empirical material.

Sexualization Just Is . . .

Consumption, according to advocates, can produce irreversible harm; as a result, safeguarding and preventative regulation are more urgent than waiting for lengthy scientific substantiation (Rush 2009: 50; see also Papadopoulos 2010). For example, Australian Emma Rush recommends using the "precautionary principle" when dealing with sexualizing media and commodities (Rush 2006, 2009). "Common sense" experience shows that these influences are dangerous and it is only a matter of time, we are told, until studies substantiate what parents and activists already know. Within this logic, waiting for proof is tantamount to child endangerment. Professor Elizabeth Handsley, Vice President of the Australian Council on Children and Media, further illustrated this conclusion in her 2008 testimony to the Australian Parliament during its inquiry into sexualization. In her statement she argued, "if we wait until there is absolute 100 per cent proof, and nobody can possibly argue anymore that there is no harm to children, the amount of harm that could possibly be done to children, in the meantime, is immeasurable" (Handsley, quoted in Rush 2009: 50). She further asserted, "We may never know for sure what affects children in what way" but it is "likely that these sorts of images and messages are harmful to children in the long term" (Handsley, quoted in Rush 2009: 50).

Falling into the trap of *petitio principii*, also known as the fallacy of begging the question, the threat of sexualization (depression, eating disorders, precocious sexual activity, and even sex work) is always already assumed in the premise and thus garners assent due to its rhetorical form rather than its substantiation. Common sense comes to replace scholarly research and thus the discourse is primarily a suppositional one. Notwithstanding, the rhetorical tone used is unequivocal and its assumptions are taken for granted as truthful. Deploying this argument is partially understandable in a context where securing human subjects' approval for conducting sexuality research with pre-adolescents and children is difficult at best and, depending on your location within the Anglophone West, almost

impossible at worst. However, the public health, communication, gender studies, sociological, historical, and childhood studies
research which complicates their conclusions is also far-too-often
absent in the literature.[3] An excellent example of this can be seen
in Emma Rush's chapter cited above. In her subsection entitled,
"Responses to critics," not a single author is cited; rather, a list of
six counterclaims (from a presumably libertarian or anti-feminist
approach) is given. Each claim (e.g., "It's simply a matter of taste"
or "It's just little girls dressing up and having fun") is followed up
with the response, "wrong" (Rush 2009: 51). Since there are no
actual quotes from any scholarly critique or popular commentator,
it is hard to take the criticisms offered by Rush as anything other
than a strawman argument set up to bolster her own proposition.

As several scholars have noted, many of the empirical claims
cited in the American Psychological Association Task Force
Report are limited because they rely upon findings which examined variables other than sexualization, but use those findings
as proof of sexualization after the fact (Egan and Hawkes 2009;
Lerum and Dworkin 2009; Veera 2009; Lumby and Albury 2010).
Levin and Kilbourne offer another example of a common practice within the sexualization literature, drawing on the voices of
parents and grandparents as primary source material (Levin and
Kilbourne 2008). As a qualitative researcher, I believe that interview material is an important and valid tool for deconstructing the
social world. Nevertheless, what I find interesting is that the narratives used draw on a one-off conception of the world, meaning
that a grandparent might discuss her granddaughter's seemingly
salacious behavior or a parent will talk about her daughter's class-
mates, but rarely is there a discussion of a daughter's activity that is
sexual. Instead, a parent might talk about a daughter feeling "fat"
or unpopular, but other key claims made within the popular literature are rarely addressed directly (Levin and Kilbourne 2008).
Given the emphasis this discourse places on sexual promiscuity,
the lack of narratives by mothers and/or girls is remarkable. This
omission could be interpreted as maternal resistance to stigmatizing a daughter's behavior. Or, it might also be seen as an indicator
that such practices might not be as common as our common sense

tells us. As I will illustrate, a review of the empirical literature supports the former and not the latter. In most popular literature on
sexualization, the voices of adults are used instead of the voices
of young girls and boys. Although a plethora of excellent ethnographic research has been done with girls and boys, this research is
conspicuously absent.

Taking the logical and empirical limitations seriously raises a host
of complicated questions about current concerns on sexualization.
Have we actually found ourselves in a contemporary context where
tween girls are ready and waiting to jump at the first chance for
oral sex with an older man? Are they unable to meet the cognitive
and relational benchmarks of their predecessors due to the effects of
self-sexualization? Are they really just a hop, skip, and a thong away
from the sex industry? Are they watching, buying, and listening
their way to a future of depressive self-destructive behavior?

Ignoring issues of methodology, data and findings of research
from a variety of disciplines is dangerous because it silences the
perspective and experiences of the very people that sexualization
activists want to protect – tweenaged girls. Moreover, it unwittingly perpetuates a political narrative that is not reflexive enough
about the implications of its assertions. I want to highlight a few
studies which offer a more complicated picture of the ways in
which young people think about and engage with sexuality and
how that intersects with current scholarship on media consumption. The claims made within the sexualization literature often
create a dystopic vision of girlhood in our contemporary culture.
For this reason, I felt it necessary to gain a better understanding of
larger demographic patterns as well as the ways in which girls make
meaning of sexuality and of their consumption of popular culture.
Tables 1.1–1.3 offer a demographic snapshot of girls' behavior,
achievement, and wellbeing in the United States, the United
Kingdom, and Australia. While these tables offer little in terms of
how girls make meaning of or negotiate the complexities of body
image, sexual violence, sexual behavior, criminality, and school
achievement, they do render visible an empirical landscape that is
far more variable and nuanced than that represented in much of the
literature on sexualization.

Table 1.1 Demographic data for girls in the United States

Female adolescent sexual behavior	Mental health/health	Educational achievement	Violent crime
Girls are waiting *longer to have sex* than before.[a,b] 43% of girls have had intercourse at least once by age 19. In 2002, the percentage was 51.1%.[b]	Mental health and other health indicators for children and teens 12–17: 4.3% depression[c]	College attainment for adults 25–34: 32% United States	Between 1990 and 2007 substantiated cases of childhood sexual abuse decreased 53%[d,e]
11% of teen girls report having sex before 15 compared to 19% in 1995. These rates mirror their European counterparts.[a]	6% learning disabilities/6% ADHD[d,e] 55% excellent health[c]	32% Australia 31% United Kingdom	During the same period physical abuse rates also declined by 52%[c]
Teen pregnancy rates[a] 39 in 1,000 births. This rate is consistent across race and ethnicity. *The lowest rate in thirty years.*			
Most common sexual practices for adolescent girls aged 14–15 in the US: Masturbation alone 40% Vaginal intercourse 11% Oral sex (to male) 12% Oral sex (to female) 2% Oral sex (by male) 10% Oral sex (by female) 1% Anal sex 4% 72% of girls who were sexually active reported their first experience with "steady partner".[a]	Obesity rates for girls (ages 2–19) in 2010: 14.5% for white girls 17.4% for Latina girls 29.2% for African American girls[c]	Degrees by gender longitudinal[f] 1972: 45,923 women 62,866 men 2011: 113,003 women 82,056 men	Sexual assault against 12–17-year-olds declined by 52% between 1993 and 2005. 7% of young women aged 18–24 who had had sex before age 20 report that their first sexual experience was involuntary.[a]
78% of girls use contraception the first time they have intercourse.[a] Currently, girls between 14 and 17 are the *most* likely group to have safe sex.[a]	Anorexia rates (2002) for teens 1%[g,h]	College success for female high-school graduates from 2003 31% Bachelors	Crime rate for adolescents: 37.8% in 1960 20.9% in 2009 Violent crime rates for tweens: 26% lower than in 1960[i]

[a] Guttmacher Institute (2011); [b] Fortenberry et al. (2010); [c] CDC (2011);
[d] Finkelhor and Jones (2006); [e] Jones and Finkelhor (2007);
[f] New England Board of Higher Education (2009);
[g] National Institute of Mental Health (2001); [h] ANRED (2008);
[i] Males and Macallair (2010).

Table 1.2 Demographic data for girls in the United Kingdom

Female adolescent sexual behavior	Mental health / health	Educational achievement	Violent crime
The median age for first sex is 16, but only 25.6% of girls (16–19) have first sex before that.[a]	Mental health and other health indicators for girls, 11–16:[c]	College attainment for adults 25–34: 32% United States	Physical violence against children in the UK actually decreased; it went from 13.1% in
In 2008, the reported UK teen pregnancy rate was 40.7 per 1,000 births while in 1998 it was 46.6 per 1,000 births.[b]	Any disorder 10.3% Anxiety disorders 5.2% Depression 1.9% Conduct disorders 5.1% Hyperkinetic disorders 0.4%	32% Australia 31% United Kingdom	1998 to 9.8% in 2009.[e] Sexual abuse also decreased; coerced sexual
Between the years 1998 and 2008 – a 10-year period – the teenage conception rate fell by 13.3% for under 18s and 11.7% for under 16s.[b]	In a 2001 study of self-assessed general health, a large majority of teenagers reported "good health."[d]		acts against those younger than 16 went from 6.8% in 1998 to 5% in 2009.[e]
Sexual acts ever experienced for girls, age 16:[f] *Non-intercourse*: No sexual acts done 47.0% Given/received oral 5.2% Given/received oral, anal 0.0%	Weight as determined by BMI for girls 2009, 16–24:[g] Underweight 9.1% Normal 51.3% Overweight 23.0% Obese 16.6% Morbidly obese 1.3%	2009 tertiary-type A graduation rates (age < 30):[i] Women 44.7% Men 35.9%	Prolonged verbal abuse, at home, school, or elsewhere, went from 14.5% in 1998 to 6% in 2009.[e]
Vaginal acts: Vaginal only 4.0% Given/received oral, vaginal 27.8% Given/received oral, vaginal, anal 6.2%	Overweight rates for different ethnicities (over 16), low income:[h]		
Out of the girls who have had sex, a majority of them, 59%, reported that their last sexual encounter was with someone they were going out with and had sex with before.[f]	Black Caribbean 69% Black African 67% Indian 56% Pakistani 63% Chinese 32% General population 38%		
Contraceptive usage has actually been increasing in recent years; right now 90% of females (16–19) use a form of contraceptive at first sex.[a]	Roughly 1% of those aged 16–18 have anorexia, with a majority of them girls.[k]	Those in full-time education at age 18:[l] Female 48% Male 42%	The British Crime Survey (2008/2009) shows violent crimes, overall, have decreased
Girls aged 16–19 were actually the *most likely* age group to use a condom during first sex within a new partnership.[j]		Those who are not in education, employment, or training:[l] Female 14% Male 16%	by roughly half (49%) since 1995.[m]

[a] Wellings et al. (2001); [b] FPA (2010); [c] Green et al. (2005); [d] Bajekal et al. (2006); [e] Radorf et al. (2011); [f] Hatherall et al. (2005); [g] Information Centre for Health and Social Care (2010); [h] Mindell and Sproston (2006); [i] OECD (2011); [j] Mercer et al. (2008); [k] Mental Health Foundation (2000); [l] Department for Education (2010); [m] Walker et al. (2009)

Table 1.3 Demographic data for girls in Australia

Female adolescent sexual behavior	Mental health/health	Educational achievement	Violent crime
Only 24.84% of girls aged 16–19 reported having sex before 16 years of age.[a]	Prevalence of mental health issues for females, 13–17 years old:[d]	College attainment for adults 25–34:	During 2007–2008, there were 7.4 substantiated child protection cases per 1,000 children.[f]
For girls aged 16–19 during 2001/2002, 23.5% reported masturbating in the past year.[b]	Attention problems 4.6% Anxious/depressed 3.6% Social problems 3.0%	32% United States 32% Australia 31% United Kingdom	Indigenous children were represented 8 times more often in child protection cases than the general population.[f]
Fertility rates, or teenage pregnancy, have decreased for girls aged 15–19; it went from 27.6 per 1,000 births in 1980 to 16.0 per 1,000 births in 2005.[c]	Asthma occurrence has actually decreased among youth aged 12–24; it went from 16% to 13% between 2001 and 2004–5.[e]		
Sexual experiences of girls, aged 16–19:[g] Vaginal intercourse 55.8% Oral sex 50.1% Anal intercourse 4.1%	Girls (general population), 15–17, and their weights 2004–5 by BMI:[e] Nearly 0% underweight Roughly 8% overweight Roughly 6% obese	National retention rates to Year 12 have increased 35% from 1980 to 2006. Retention rate for Year 12 in 2006:[e] Males 69% Females 81%	Those 16–19-year-olds who reported being forced or frightened into doing something sexually:[g] Men 2.8% Women 16.1%
93.8% of girls aged 16–19 believed that they should not have sex with someone who is not their regular partner.[a]	This is lower than males of the same age, roughly 16% of whom are overweight. Indigenous girls, 15–17, by BMI during 2004–5:[e] Underweight not available Overweight 12.2% Obese 7.5%	A large majority of students in Year 7 (aged 12–14) actually met reading, writing, and numeracy benchmarks (91%, 94%, and 82% respectively).[e]	Sexual assault rates were worse for those aged 10–14 than 0–9, and girls were three-quarters of reported victims.[f]
Contraceptive usage during first intercourse has actually increased significantly; men and women in the 1950s had a less than 30% usage rate, while in modern times it is over 90%.[a]	Only 1% (1 in 100) of adolescent girls develop anorexia nervosa.[h]	Those aged 20–24 engaging in study leading to a bachelors degree:[e] Men 51.2% Women: 63.7%	Juvenile crime rates in Australia went from 4,092 per 1,000,000 juveniles in 1995–6 to 3,023 in 2003–4.[i] 68% of young people in juvenile detention had a history of abuse or neglect.[i] While 10 in every 100,000 males aged 17 were a prisoner in 2007, the number of females was so low it was found to be statistically insignificant.[j]

[a] Rissel et al. (2007); [b] Richters et al. (2007); [c] Australian Bureau of Statistics (2007);
[d] Sawyer et al. (2000); [e] Australian Institute of Health and Welfare (2007);
[f] Australian Institute of Health and Welfare (2009); [g] de Visser et al. (2007);
[h] Eating Disorders Victoria (n.d.); [i] Justice Action Australia (2011);
[j] Australian Institute of Criminology (2006).

Data from the recent National Survey of Sexual Health and Behavior offer a distinctly different perspective from the one found in the sexualization literature I have reviewed thus far (Herbenick et al. 2010). Although the sample surveyed did not include the youngest of tweens, the answers provided by young people between the ages of 14 and 18 in the United States are telling to say the least. Far and away, masturbation was the most common sexual practice among 14–15-year-old teens; 62% of boys and 40% of girls are engaging in this form of solitary autoeroticism. Moreover, only 12% of boys and 10% of girls claimed to have received oral sex from an opposite sex partner, whereas only 1% of girls and boys reported receiving oral sex from a same sex partner (Herbenick et al. 2010). Hardly the new goodnight kiss or a common entrepreneurial practice, oral sex is relatively rare and, although the rates are not the same for boys and girls, clearly both sexes are giving and receiving. The response rate for vaginal and anal intercourse was equally low (9% of boys and 11% of girls had vaginal intercourse in the last 12 months while 1% of boys and 4% of girls engaged in anal sex) (Herbenick et al. 2010). Researchers from the Center for Sexual Health also found that when young people (between the ages of 14 and 17) have vaginal intercourse, they are the *most* responsible when it comes to safer sex practices (79.1% of males and 58.1% of females used a condom in their last ten acts of intercourse – rates for anal sex were unspecified) (Fortenberry et al. 2010). The Center for Disease Control's "National Youth Risk Behavior Survey," which focuses on young people in grades 9 through 12 in the United States, revealed similar downward trends in onset of first vaginal intercourse and an increase in condom use (CDC 2011). Departing from the sexualization literature which claims that media and commodities produce an unyielding desire for promiscuity, the CDC found a marked decrease in teens who said they had slept with four or more people over their lifetime (from 18.7% in 1991 to 13.8% in 2009). Alcohol and drug consumption prior to intercourse has also declined between 2001 and 2009 (from 25.6% to 21.6%) (CDC 2011).

Public health surveys in Britain such as the National Survey of

Sexual Attitudes and Lifestyles and the longitudinal survey with heterosexual teens in Scotland entitled SHARE have revealed equally interesting results (Wight and Henderson 2004). While the age of first intercourse in the United Kingdom has dropped in the past 30 years from 17 to 16, the frequency of sexual experiences involving intercourse was very low (Wight and Henderson 2004). Of the adolescents who reported having intercourse (37% by age 16), 58% did so less than ten times and another 34% reported having intercourse three times or less over the past year (Wight and Henderson 2004). In his review of public health data in the United States two decades earlier, Mike Males showed that neither male nor female adolescents were out mimicking *Girls Gone Wild* videos or MTV; rather, sexual intercourse between heterosexual youth had risen only 7% for boys and 6% for girls over a 22-year period (between 1970 and 1992) (Males 1996).

Sharon Lamb's insightful research with girls suggests that, "girls, like boys, are deeply sexual, and deeply aggressive creatures. And these impulses exist alongside their sweetness, competence and ability to love and care for others" (Lamb 2001: 9). As the narratives she collected attest, the sexuality of girls is a "complex" manifestation of the social, the subjective, and the psychic; a mode of being that falls outside of the reductionist binary of innocent/ sexual (Lamb 2001: 8; see also Epstein et al. 2003; Robinson and Davies 2008; Taylor 2010). Emma Renold's groundbreaking work with British youth, and Louisa Allen's in New Zealand, both illustrate the manifold ways in which boys and girls make meaning of sexuality, sexual embodiment, and identity (Renold 2005; Allen 2005). The young people in these studies refuse simple classifications of victims or agents; rather, they experience pleasure and disembodiment, are relational and selfish, enforce and challenge problematic ideologies of gender, sex, and sexuality, and most times, like their adult counterparts, find themselves stuck in the dense thicket of desire and social expectation (see also Fine and McClelland 2006; Tolman 2005; Fine 1998). Recent ethnographic work by Jessica Ringrose and Emma Renold with Welsh girls who were asked to make meaning of the Slut Walk in their town reveal just how nuanced tweenagers and teenagers are in discussions of sexual politics (Renold and Ringrose 2011; see also Renold and Ringrose 2008).

Similarly, the Kaiser Foundation found that young people's sexual decision making was far more reflexive than the writing on sexualization presumes (Kaiser Foundation 2003). When surveyed about why they were not having sex, 43% of 14–18-year-olds said they wanted to wait until they were in a committed relationship. The majority of teens also felt that delaying sex relations helped them stay in control of a relationship (91%) and insured the respect of parents (91%) and friends (84%) (Kaiser Foundation 2003). Many did not want to worry about pregnancy and/or STDs (79%) (Kaiser Foundation 2003). Equally complex were the reasons for having sex, which ranged from curiosity (85%), love (69%), and feeling like the time was right (82%), to hoping it would make a relationship closer (70%), wanting to get it over with (58%), and being under the influence (18%) (Kaiser Foundation 2003). These findings should not deny the challenges or difficulties associated with sexual decision making or the ways in which gendered pressure or homophobia can become a significant factor in such activities (Shucksmith 2004). Rather, it illustrates the multifaceted context within which young people make such choices.

Overall media consumption among both tweens and teens is on the rise; however, recent longitudinal data reveal that sexually inexperienced young people between the ages of 14 and 18 watch more media than their sexually active peers, but that their consumption of specific programs differs (sexually active teens are more likely to watch cable television and other adult-oriented programs) (Bersamin et al. 2010). Nevertheless, as David Buckingham and Sara Bragg note, what is unclear in many media effects studies is the manner in which young people make sense of or "read" the media and how it shapes their perception of self, sex, and identity (Buckingham and Bragg 2004; see also Buckingham 2000). While there can be no doubt that sexual content in the media has increased over the years, sociologist Karen Sternheimer notes that one should not assume that all children interpret its content in the same manner (Sternheimer 2003). Sternheimer argues that researchers need to take context, gender, race, and sexuality into account (Sternheimer 2003; see also Buckingham and Bragg 2004; Egan 2012). What studies have shown is that consumption of media is neither completely idiosyncratic nor monolithic (Celeste Kearney 2006; Attwood 2011; Jackson and Westrupp 2010; Jackson 2011; Bragg et al. 2012). Although media may, in fact, make some young people feel pressured to have sex, it may make others more sexually responsible in terms of condom use, and for others it might provide a positive site of affirmation for sexual desire. Could media produce a multitude of complex and at times contradictory feelings for the same person?

Angela McRobbie argues that the postfeminist media land-scape within which young girls find themselves offers increasingly narrow representations and thus sites of identification in terms of gender and sexuality (McRobbie 2009). Marnina Gonick further argues that constructions of girl power forward messages of sassy individualism, self-pleasure, and being ready for sex and sexuality (Gonick 2006). Such postfeminist constructions are deeply seduc-tive, but ultimately problematic for Gonick and McRobbie; their mix of consumption, hegemonic femininity, and neoliberalism absents inequality and nullifies political and social change (Gonick 2006; McRobbie 2009). Rosalind Gill's research sheds light on the pressures young people feel when faced with an onslaught of sexual representations as well as the ways in which such representations may foster disidentification, complex reading, and outright rejec-tion (Gill 2007, 2009). Feona Attwood foregrounds the profundity of sex and sexualization within our postmodern media landscape, but insightfully notes that the word "sexualization" is a flimsy one due to its inability to accurately describe the complex practices of media and media consumption in our current culture (Attwood 2006).

Ethnographic research with tweens in New Zealand and Australia illustrates the nuanced and, at times, contradictory reading of sexual advice and sexual representations found in magazines for young people (Jackson and Westrupp 2010; Mulholland 2011). Monique Mulholland found that girls and boys often expressed indifference as opposed to shock or titillation in their consumption of such images. However, this seemingly blasé attitude did not translate into more open attitudes regarding gender and sexuality – both boys and girls deployed slut-bashing narratives in their discussions of girls and sexuality (Mulholland 2011). Research conducted by Sue Jackson and Elizabeth Westrupp shows that, for girls, postfeminist magazines fostered knowledge about a variety of sexual practices, and that girls often positioned themselves in complex ways in terms of such practices. What was more worrisome was the heteronormativity or "heterosexual address" of such magazines and the "highly limited" ways in which femininity and girlhood were represented (Jackson and Westrupp 2010: 374). Ultimately they conclude "in preference to drawing the focus on the regulation of girls (yet again) it would seem rather more useful at this point to widen the lens to how magazines like *Girlfriend* conceptualize their readership and whether and how they engage with contemporary debates about sexual media and young girls" (Jackson and Westrupp 2010: 374).

In their conversations with British tweens, David Buckingham and Sara Bragg found that girls and boys were skeptical of advertisements, television, and magazines and at times forwarded an almost moralistic vision of the sex portrayed within these media sources – particularly when discussing the dangers it could pose to younger viewers (people 1–3 years younger than themselves) (Buckingham and Bragg 2004). Children were not passive readers of media texts – they questioned storylines, discussed the credibility of claims, and criticized the actions of celebrities as well as the practices of the reporters and photographers who wrote about and photographed them (Buckingham and Bragg 2004). Later research, conducted with parents and children and funded by the Equal Opportunities Committee of the Scottish Parliament which was then translated into the Scottish Parliamentary Report, highlighted similar complexities in the reading of media and products deemed sexualized or sexualizing (Buckingham et al. 2010; Bragg et al. 2012). It is noteworthy that of all the governmental reports written in the UK, this is the only one authored by experts in the field (Buckingham et al. 2010).[4] Although a common sentiment expressed in the literature is that the common viewer is unable to critically engage with messages and representations found within sexualized media, this was not the case for Scottish parents and/or children. As Sarah Bragg states when discussing method and findings,

> we prepared in advance some statements about sexualization, intended to prompt debate and focused on what we imagined might be neglected "complex" ideas; we never needed to use them, since the issues were invariably – and better – covered during discussions of relevant experiences. In some ways, then, we *under*estimated the capacities of participants, and *over*estimated the uniqueness of the insights generated by academic analysis; the two proved closer than we anticipated (Bragg et al. 2012).

These insights render problematic the oft repeated suppositions, that adults and children are unable to distinguish "fantasy from fiction" or offer a critical and complex read of media content. It also renders suspect the belief that most parents are alarmed and ready for action – claims which are presented as self-evidently true in the two Home Office reports (Bragg et al. 2012).

Drawing on three case studies in the United Kingdom, Emma Renold and Jessica Ringrose highlight the anti-linear model of consumption girls employ in their use of sexualized images (Renold and Ringrose 2011). Analyzing the use of visual symbols (e.g., the playboy bunny) or particular words, songs, or poetry on Bebo (a social networking site), they argue that girls embody multiple "becomings . . . that complicate the binary logic of sexual victim/sexual empowerment and sexual innocence/sexual excess" to reveal the nuanced way in which girls navigate the push and pull of "gendered sexual innocence and (hetero)sexual subject/objectification" (Renold and Ringrose 2011: 402). Exploring consumption in this way allowed Renold and Ringrose to "connect up girls' feelings of pleasure and power in the becoming-sexual-woman with their experiences of virtual and embodied networks colonized with real and symbolic (hetero)sexualized violence in their everyday lives" (Renold and Ringrose 2011: 402).

Mark Lipton's research analyzes how queer youth critically read and reinscribe popular media to find a place of representation within it (Lipton 2008). Lipton shows that "the queer imagination helps queer youth find strong moral guidance in a media world where queerness is absent" (Lipton 2008: 173). Research conducted by Dionne Stephens and April Few with pre-adolescent African American girls further illustrates the complexity involved in media consumption. Stephens and Few examined how young girls interpret and make meaning of hip hop videos (Stephens and Few 2007). In interviews girls were able to interpret and identify dominant sexual scripts (e.g., gold digger, baby mama, or earth mother) within hip hop music videos, but that their consumption of these messages was anything but neutral. Most of the pre-adolescents were deeply critical of the women in the videos who were sexually promiscuous or fell outside of more socially acceptable feminine roles (Stephens and Few 2007). In this regard, hip hop videos served as cautionary tales for how not to behave instead of how-to manuals for future behavior (see also Jackson 2011; Mulholland 2011; Ringrose and Renold 2011). Media consumption is a more complex and dynamic process that involves more than the simple transmission and indoctrination of unmediated ideological messages; rather, its contents and values are used, reframed and even rejected by viewers (Buckingham 2008; Jerslev 2008). To this end, reading media, sexual and otherwise, is a deeply nuanced experience that is shaped by pleasure, loathing, boredom, biography, and culture.

Conclusion

As I have illustrated throughout this chapter, the peril of sexualization is said to foster not only the desire to look like, but also the compulsion to act like the celebrities featured on television, in magazines, and in the music industry (Rush and La Nauze 2006a; APA 2007; Levin and Kilbourne 2008; Farley 2009a, 2009b; M. Hamilton 2009a; Klein 2009). According to advocates, objectification is particularly insidious because consumption creates an almost alchemical reaction; it transgresses and transforms the normative boundaries of biology, psychology, and cognition.

Destroying childhood itself, something almost monstrous is left in its wake – a self-involved, cognitively impaired, mentally ill, and hypersexual tween who revels in her own subjugation and longs for the lap dance couch (APA 2007; Farley 2009; M. Hamilton 2009a; Magner and Hall 2009; Papadopoulos 2010; Dines 2011). She may seek out sex with older men or casual sex with numerous partners, and may suffer from eating disorders, depression, and the inability to engage in caring relationships with others (Hymowitz 2002; Farley 2009a, 2009b; Klein 2009). She likes "skanky" clothes and "fuck me shoes" – she is neither child nor adult, but a disturbing mix of rampant promiscuity in newly pubescent (or soon to be pubescent) body (Rivenbark 2006; Hamilton 2007; Oppliger 2008). We are told that sexualizing materials are ever present, and as noxious as poisoned air, thus avoiding their influence seems almost impossible – however, their risks seem to threaten a specific type of girlhood (white, middle-class and heterosexual). In fact, it is the escalating danger posed by this phenomenon that necessitates adult intervention and, for some, prohibition (Rush and La Nauze 2006a, 2006b; APA 2007; Durham 2008; Levin and Kilbourne 2008; Papadopoulos 2010). She is emblematic of innocence transformed, and, once sexualized, a pathologized and deviant subject in need of help due to her contagious quality (Duits and van Zoonen 2011).

This argument relies upon and reproduces a longstanding Anglophone presumption of the danger of exposing the sexual instinct to harmful cultural influences (Laqueur 1990; Evans 1991; Mort 2000; Hawkes 2004). The sexual instinct is conceptualized as fragile in nature and highly combustible; once ignited, it becomes compulsive and poses a threat to the individual and the broader social order. Compulsive masturbation after reading salacious materials, or deviant sexual practices emerging as a result of comic books, television, music lyrics, or the Internet – anxiety surrounding the sway and impact of these negative influences has compelled Anglophone activists, academics, and politicians to craft policies, organize boycotts, and enact prohibition against everything from fiction for children in the early eighteenth century to recent calls for banning video games and "lad mags." These discourses presume the instability of our sexual instinct which must be brought under control and subsequently normalized by a moral, medical, or psychological expert (Foucault 1980; Evans 1991; Hawkes 2004; Egan and Hawkes 2010). Nevertheless, it is noteworthy that, within the literature reviewed thus far, popular culture takes on the persona of a sexual predator and its effects are presumed to be unyielding.

It is the sexual nature of its content and its gendered messages that make its impact exponentially greater than other more positive sources that are equally ubiquitous (religious, medical, or psychological messages). Sex magnifies the product and its effects, thereby setting off a chain reaction in the body. Notwithstanding, even within the logic of antisexualization narratives, sexualization cannot be totalitarian in its function, else critique and intervention would be impossible. As Linda Duits and Lisbet van Zoonen argue, "the media" is anything but monolithic, and the proliferation of form and content produced in this sense makes the postmodern media landscape radically different from the one under analysis by scholars such as Horkheimer and Adorno and more recently by radical feminists in the 1970s (Duits and van Zoonen 2011).

This paradoxical position (that sexualization is everywhere and unyielding but advocates have somehow escaped its influence and can help you fix the situation) is taken for granted within sexualization narratives. The impact of intercession should be minimal at best and futile at worst. Equally important, because agency, resistance, or even partial consent is rendered impossible for girls, all are doomed, and as a result the campaign against sexualization gets further entrenched within its paradoxical position. The discourse on sexualization unwittingly creates a vision of girlhood that can only ever be damaged, sexualized, and self-subjugating (see also Duschinsky 2010, 2011). This position is ultimately untenable because it invalidates the very premise of the movement itself.

How can activists give parents instruction on "what they can do about sexualization" (some variation on this theme is the subtitle of most books on sexualization) if intervention is implausible in the first place? Might this paradox, as well as the deep disconnect between claims within the literature and the empirical picture, point to the fact that, although this discourse is about girlhood, it is also about something else? I argue that the discourse on sexualization is only partially about its manifestly stated goals. Deconstructing the various historical threads at work in this discourse and the deployment of affect reveals that this discourse and the figures of the girl child (as both sexualized and innocent) are actually displacements or metaphors for larger cultural and socio-economic instabilities emblematic of our postmodern or hypermodern epoch. In this sense, they are also a reflection of an Anglophone cultural unconscious and an attempt to suture that which has been wounded (middle-class security, Western supremacy, as well as distinctions of age and gender as identities of difference). The sexualized child is a potent (and possibly a seductive) figure whose supposed actions and subjectivity reveal the fissures of gender, sexuality, race, class, and age – a monstrous outcome that must be brought under control.

2

(Hetero)Sexualization, Pathological Femininity, and Hope for the Future

One example of this [sexual] aggression recently played out at a local private school, where it was charmingly dubbed "robbing the cradle." Two senior girls each solicited a freshman boy for sexual purposes by wearing a T-shirt to school with "I want (boy's name)" on it. It created quite a stir and bestowed some status on the younger boys in question. It also puts parents on alert that in our sexually predatory culture, parents also need to worry about safeguarding their boys from the girls, not just vice versa.

> Patricia Dalton (2005) "Class is out and trash is in"

Introduction

Reading Patricia Dalton's diagnosis on the state of tween and teen girlhood, one comes away with a sense of foreboding, a feeling that young girls may have actually gone wild, enacting the excesses of a hypersexual culture. Whereas before women used to complain about objectification and being reduced to their appearance; today "grrrrrrls" are "*volunteering* to be sex objects" in an attempt to "bypass girlhood" and proceed directly to womanhood (Dalton 2005). When parental guidance is lacking (we are told that fathers should "take the lead in setting limits on their daughters' dress"), girls get seduced by sexualizing messages and become both sexually compulsive and psychologically damaged (Dalton 2005). Seeking sexy above humility and monogamy, girls want to be more like Samantha from *Sex in the City* than "Audrey Hepburn" (Dalton 2005). The "increasing aggressive sexual behavior" of girls has become so pervasive that parents are advised to "worry about safeguarding their boys" (Dalton 2005). The "problem with kids today," according to Dalton, is clearly gender specific. While it might be tempting to throw one's hands up in surrender, Dalton reminds us to be hopeful because "there is often a lost girl" underneath it all (Dalton 2005).

Nancy Leigh DeMoss, author of *Lies Young Women Believe* and *Becoming A Woman of Discretion: Cultivating a Pure Heart in a Sensual World*, paints a similar picture when discussing the risks and impacts of our sex-saturated immodest culture (DeMoss 2011; see also DeMoss 2003, 2008). Girls are taught to "be brazen, to be forward, to display themselves and their bodies in ways that are designed to get sexual attention, to be the center of attraction" (DeMoss 2011; see also DeMoss 2003, 2008). Like her other neo-conservative counterparts, DeMoss seeks solutions to these problems in the pedagogy of abstinence, the promotion of parental responsibility, and in religiously inspired fashion campaigns such as the popular "modeling modesty" (DeMoss 2011). Although remedies may differ, the warnings forwarded by DeMoss resonate with some popular feminist literature on the topic. For example, Jean Kilbourne cautions that, although "tight T-shirts for little girls saying 'so many boys, so little time'" may seem unimportant, or even "clever," parents will "cease to think that when their [daughter] becomes sexually active at 12. There is huge pressure on girls to look sexy and dress provocatively at a younger and younger age and boys are getting graphic sexualised messages" (Kilbourne, quoted in Womack 2007). In both, clothing contaminates and portends future promiscuous action.

Close reading of the sexualization literature from both the left and the right also reveals that the range of concern is often limited to the bodies and practices of girls who are heterosexual,

Figure 2.1 This poster (year unknown), produced by Social Purity advocates and later used by the American Sexual Hygiene movement, illustrates how purity campaigners deployed a similar logic in their cautionary tales on the dangers of salacious materials in the life of the girl child. Once ingested, sexual materials set the path for life; embracing a "fast life" led to the rejection of acceptable femininity, maternity, and brought dejection later in life. Nevertheless, it is important to note that these materials produced similar results in boys. As I noted elsewhere with Gail Hawkes, purity reform was, in part, a response to the disquiet over the rise of urbanization (Egan and Hawkes 2007, 2010). Concerned with immigration and dysgenics, sexual hygienists in the Anglophone West focused their energies on habituating middle-class values of stable and monogamous heterosexuality in working-class children (Egan and Hawkes 2010). In a similar fashion, the girl child in the sexualization literature is emblematic of a much larger set of adult insecurities regarding the future of the heterosexual family.

Source: Wikimedia Commons

white, middle-class, and at risk of violating dominant conceptions of gender, age, and comportment. As a result, the issue becomes one of gender and sexual abhorrence as opposed to a critique of structural inequity and sexist gender stereotypes represented in the media, which may explain why an undercurrent of disgust and anxiety is often present in the literature. In other words, instead of deconstructing problematic representations of gender, sexuality, and race in media aimed at young people, advocates focus on the problems associated with a particular type of deviant or "phallic" femininity (Rush and La Nauze 2006a, 2006b; Durham 2008; Levin and Kilbourne 2008; Oppliger 2008; Farley 2009a, 2009b; M. Hamilton 2009a, 2009b; McRobbie 2009; Ryan 2010; Carey 2011; Dines 2011; Levin 2011). The problem becomes one of sexual practices, not sexism, racism, and homophobia. How does this vision get naturalized within the literature? There is no simple answer to this question; it cannot and should not be reduced to a case of moral panic. Although it is limited, the discourse does highlight a particularly troubling landscape of sexualized representation; however, all too often it gets transformed into pathological classifications and moralizing proscriptions. In the worst cases, "healthy" alternatives come to function as normalizing devices that delimit a girl and her sexuality into narrow and, at times, deeply conservative parameters, compelled by the anxieties of middle-class advocates rather than by an ethic of sexual citizenship (Egan and Hawkes 2009). Teasing apart the various ways in which gender, race, and sexuality are used in the construction of the sexualized girl will shed light on how and why the problem often *feels so real*. This chapter critically interrogates how the sexualized girl is rendered intelligible and becomes a metaphor for cultural disquiet surrounding family, gender, and the future of feminism itself.

Babes in Boyland: Producing the Phallic Tween

In *The Aftermath of Feminism*, Angela McRobbie argues that the face of patriarchy and inequality has changed in our contemporary postfeminist epoch (McRobbie 2009). Unlike backlash politics, which repudiate the goals of gender equality, "postfeminism can be equated with a double movement, [because] gender retrenchment is secured, paradoxically through the wide dissemination of discourses of female freedom" (McRobbie 2009: 62). Within this context, girls are fed the message that they are free to achieve anything, and as such, any lack of success is the result of individual failure. However, when reviewing issues of poverty, job inequality, and violence, one sees rather quickly that it is only a masquerade of freedom and success that is on offer for young women (McRobbie 2009). In a strange twist of logic, McRobbie departs from a more structural assessment to argue that the phallic girl, and the type of behavior and sense of subjectivity she inspires, is emblematic of this shift in contemporary culture. Her description of phallic femininity captures many of the assumptions and feelings at work in more popular rhetoric on sexualization.

Phallic femininity is a market-driven and politically inert version of sexual equality. In popular media, phallic females are bawdy, resistive, and as sexually liberated as their male counterparts. They like "exhibitionism, lap dances, casual sex, pornography, and drinking like the boys" but make sure to remain "feminine enough" to retain their place on the dating market block (McRobbie 2009: 83). The phallic girl ensures "gender re-stabilization" because she not only capitulates to the demands of the beauty complex and masculine desire, but she also seems to celebrate them (McRobbie 2009: 84). Seeking to emulate the phallic girls represented on reality television, girls engage in the worst kinds of male behavior. For McRobbie, emulation is the reason the enactment of phallic femininity is more problematic than the issue of representation. Although certain celebrities may cash in on this as a persona, for the ordinary girl this means something quite different, "drinking to excess, getting into fights . . . wearing very short skirts, high heels, and skimpy tops, having casual sex, often passing out on the street and having to be taken home by friends or by the police" (McRobbie 2009: 85). Girls and young women seem to follow this behavior in lockstep fashion and uncritically embrace its ethos which is why resistance or political challenge is viewed as short-lived, inert, or commercialized. McRobbie's description of phallic femininity is a deeply evocative, almost dystopian, account of monstrous outcomes and the death of feminism. It is also a significant departure from her other writing because it ignores ethnographic and demographic findings on the actual behavior of girls and young women. While many of McRobbie's insights are provocative, her descriptions of phallic femininity too often feel like invectives against women and girls who violate feminist femininity and middle-class comportment by embracing exhibitionism and patriarchal norms.

Former head of the left-leaning Australia Institute, Clive Hamilton, offers another example of this type of thinking when he states that the "boorish" behavior of girls should come as no surprise in a cultural context where living "out of control" has become the new normal (C. Hamilton 2009: 90). Gender equality is now equated with behaving "as badly as boys" and associated with a new category of gender, "girls with balls" (C. Hamilton 2009: 90).[1] Indiscriminate with sex as they are with drink and drugs, girls "capitulat[e] to every desire;" nevertheless, we are warned that such surfeit always comes with a cost – a lonely and unhappy life (C. Hamilton 2009: 91). Hamilton emphasizes that girls must learn that, "we cannot be free if we become slaves to our [sexual] passions," which is why sexual restraint offers more, not less, freedom (C. Hamilton 2009: 91). There may be a glimmer of hope on the horizon – Hamilton states that a new cultural norm is emerging where being good is the new cool. Once this shift gains enough traction, bad girls will end up where they belong – socially sanctioned and marginalized.

American psychologist Melissa Farley's vision of the future is far less hopeful. Farley believes that "prostitution behaviors" are "what it means to be female today" – which is why girls seek out self-objectification and self-degradation (Farley 2009a: 119; Farley 2009b: 146). When "femaleness is commodified" girls are valued for their "sexual characteristics alone" and *de facto* get "transformed into prostitutes" (Farley 2009b: 146). According to Farley, girls succumb to the prostitutization of femininity or what she terms "a hypersexualized prostitution-like version of themselves" which infects their subjectivity and spurs action (Farley 2009a: 119). As others have noted, outcomes intensify with exposure – precocious sex, self-degradation, eating disorders, and other pathological ideas invade "every aspect of their *hosts' lives*, robbing them of any remaining vestiges of self confidence or happiness, compromising every organ and system in their bodies, and causing emotional, spiritual, and mental torment" (Maines 2009: 73, *emphasis added*). American psychologist Sharon Olfman further cautions that little girls who are "sexualized – dressed in a belly shirt with a provocative phrase written across the backside of her shorts, her lips glossed and her hair streaked" are being damaged by a "soul-destroying script" that will lead to low self-esteem, eating disorders, or worse (Olfman 2009: 2).

During a recent presentation at the *Right 2 Childhood Conference* in Sydney, Australia, psychologist Joe Tucci warned participants that children "who can't even tie their shoelaces yet" are "displaying aberrant sexual behaviour" such as public masturbation, sexual assault, and sexualized play (Tucci, quoted in Rowlands 2011). Although one might be wary about collapsing sexual assault and sexualized play within the same category, Tucci's assertions further highlight the central argument put forward by many anti-sexualization authors – that sexualization infects girlhood and reconstitutes it into something deviant and, worse, contagious (Tucci, quoted in Rowlands 2011). The stated psychopathological outcomes of sexualization are most clearly illustrated in a recent diagnostic invention created by the American education scholar Diane Levin: compassion deficit disorder (Levin, quoted in Andrews 2011). Levin argues that because sexualization "treats individuals as dehumanised objects, and sex and sexual behaviour out of the context of a caring human relationship," it undermines "the foundation children need to grow up to have healthy relationships or sex" and, as a result, causes compassion deficit disorder (Levin, quoted in Andrews 2011). Compassion deficit disorder impedes the child's ability to "become [a] fully functional human being who can participate in caring and just relationships;" those who suffer from this disorder are unable to "empathize with others or to relate to others with mutual care, affection and a sense of fairness and justice" (Levin 2011: 30; see also Levin 2008). Within this model, consumption creates a careless, hedonistic, and narcissistic creature who is less than fully human.

Readers are warned that our cultural conceptions of girls as somehow more docile, well behaved, and empathetic need to be radically revised, because they are outmoded at best and delusional at worst (M. Hamilton 2009a, 2009b). For female tweens, sex "is increasingly casual and random" and romantic scripts no longer hold any value (M. Hamilton 2009b: 152). Whereas in the past boys might have complained about not getting to second base with a girl – today girls are as sexually voracious and aggressive as their male counterparts and are more likely to make "the first move" (M. Hamilton 2009b: 152). As a result, a boy's "heartfelt gestures" and desire "for more genuine relationships" are being "passed over" by girls who are more interested in reality television and raunch than romance (M. Hamilton 2009b: 155). Emphasizing just how appalling things have become, Maggie Hamilton notes that, although many girls want to maintain their virginity, they are more than willing to engage in oral sex because it falls outside the classification of "sex" (M. Hamilton 2009b: 152). The outcome of such behavior is a lonely, desperate, and defeated future (M. Hamilton 2009b; see also Levin and Kilbourne 2008; Oppliger 2008; Reist 2009a; Walter 2010; Carey 2011).

Popular Cultures

Within the literature, a girl's subjectivity is permeable, but only to sexually corrosive messages; any other narrative – romance, sport, science fiction, religion, magic, art, patriotism, music, basically anything that is not sexualizing – is less persuasive and less catalytic. We are told that it is the ubiquity of sexualizing messages and the lack of diversity within popular culture that makes the situation so powerful and dire. Reviewing Nielsen's[2] consumption ratings for the 2011–12 US network broadcast season, one sees that *Glee*, *American Idol* (competition and results), *Family Guy*, *The Cleveland*

Show, and *X Factor* topped the list for teenage viewers (there was no data available on 8–12-year-olds) (Adalian 2012). Competition shows, cartoons, and a high-school musical seem to capture the imagination. Sex and/or sexiness are featured in these shows; however, they are not particularly salacious. A critical review of the media landscape also reveals that the concept of "popular media" is far more complicated than it was 40 years ago. Unlike the past, where two or three networks controlled all the programming, the rise of cable television and the Internet has fragmented the concept of the popular. The ever increasing sources of media young people have access to as well as the variety of messaging found therein (including those messages created by young people themselves) highlight that what the media tells us is more complex and variegated than it was before (Sternheimer 2003). Moreover, there are also cable networks which feature religious, sports, romance, news, mystery, medical, and/or true crime programming 24 hours a day that can be viewed on television or online. Communication scholars Linda Duits and Lisbet van Zoonen (2011) argue that the discourse on sexualization ignores the terrain of media practices and the variety of role models with whom girls identify. While the venues for accessing or even accidentally stumbling upon pornography are numerous and it is true that the media is more sexualized, it is important to remember that reception is highly complicated and rarely straightforward (Attwood 2006, 2009; Family Lives 2012). One only has to examine Facebook, memes, websites, blogs, zines, etc., to understand just how diverse the nature of information and entertainment has become (Duits and van Zoonen 2011).

The multibillion-dollar success of *The Twilight Saga* or *The Hunger Games* and the gender and sexual ideologies they forward also seem to fall on deaf ears or have little or no impact within the sexualization literature (Grossman 2009; Hala 2009).[3] One might wonder why the "true love waits" narrative (and its pronatalist and anti-abortion presumptions) of *Twilight* is so inert and only tropes of sexualization which objectify, dehumanize, and eradicate empathy function in such a singular and causal fashion. Notwithstanding the intergenerational sex (Edward is, after all, almost 100 years older), the sticky wicket of monogamy (Edward versus Jacob), and the overbearing nature of chivalry presented in *Twilight*, why not an addiction to chivalrous patriarchy and stringent sexual ideologies instead of "so many boys so little time" and compassion deficit disorder? Given the popularity of the Katniss character and her actions in *The Hunger Games*, why not fears over the desire for anarchism and anti-authoritarianism instead of phallic femininity and exhibitionism? One might infer that for most people (including most anti-sexualization advocates), it would seem outlandish to grant these stories that level of influence and impact. However, such logic is often uncritically deployed in discussions of sexualized consumption.

If we revisit the vast amount of research on girls discussed in chapter 1, we see that girls have an ambivalent relationship to media and popular culture, one that is both pleasurable and painful, fun and constraining, beset by confusion and boredom, and, although sexualizing images may be resisted by girls, it does not mean they are unaffected either (Walkerdine 1998; Rand 2003; Buckingham and Bragg 2004; Willett 2005; Lipton 2008; Renold and Ringrose 2008, 2011; Gill 2009; Jackson and Westrupp 2010; Jackson and Vares 2011; Mulholland 2011; Vares et al. 2011; Bragg et al. 2012; Ringrose 2013). Girls feel pressured and angry, and sometimes both. They are neither free agents nor automatons – rather, they find their way through and get stuck in the dense thicket of ideology. They are weighed down and find joy in parental expectation, peer groups, and popular culture, and experience pleasure, as well as pain, in the secret garden of personal preference. They are subject to, subject others to, and subvert conservative gender and sexual ideologies (McRobbie and Nava 1984; McRobbie 1991; Mitchell and Reid-Walsh 2005; Renold 2005; Malik 2005; Renold and Ringrose 2008; Ringrose 2008, 2010; Willis 2009; Jackson 2011). Their sexual practices and sexual cultures are complicated, confusing, and confounding, as well as pleasurable and complex (Fine 1998; Lamb 2001; Epstein et al. 2003; Rasmussen 2004; Allen 2005; Paechter 2009; Gosine 2008; CDC 2011). It would be inaccurate to say that media has no impact, but the claims made by sexualization authors are rendered suspect when weighed against the vast terrain of empirical literature.

Corrupted, Passive, and Single-Minded?

Enmeshed in a totalizing ideological form, we are also told that girls have become narcissistic, compliant, and self-sexualizing subjects. Because reception is hypodermic and is said to transform cognitive, sexual, and emotional registers, resistance is both absent and futile. This begs the question, is this actually the case? Reviewing recent protests against sexual violence with the Slut Walk, the increasing support for gay marriage, as well as various critical websites and blogs such as Scarleteen, Spark a Movement, the Crunk Feminist Collective, the Queer Youth Project, and the Black Youth Project (to name only a few), renders their supposition regarding political critique suspect at best and erroneous at worst (www.queeryouth-project.com; www.sparksummit.com; crunkfeministcollective. wordpress.com; www.scarleteen.com; www.blackyouthproject. com). Examining these blogs and videos, one sees that young people are *challenging* popular cultural representations and the sexist, racist, and homophobic ideologies underpinning everything from the criminal justice system and media coverage (what does and does not get covered) to sexual violence and the manipulation of photographs in teen magazines. Political strategies involve media making and social networking sites such as Facebook and Twitter as much as they do collective in-person demonstrations.[4]

During the writing of this chapter, several YouTube videos went viral that further illustrate how political contestation may be different, but it is not absent. The videos included: a 15-year-old boy, Jonah Mowry,[5] talking about his experiences with homophobic bullying, a video which inspired many young gay men to respond with videos of how they lived through that experience. Several young girls (e.g., "Dear Jonah Mowry") also responded with their experiences with slut bashing and bullying. In other posts, a 13-year-old girl talked about slut shaming and why it is problematic; the "S$#T white girls say" video and its various memes (which have spanned issues as far-reaching as racism, classism, transphobia, homophobia, and whorephobia) went viral; and the *It Gets Better Campaign* gained in popularity.[6] Most recently,

14-year-old Julia Bluhm spearheaded a successful campaign against the popular US-based magazine, *Seventeen*; after getting messages from 80,000 individuals, the editor agreed to stop airbrushing and manipulating the images of their models and to showcase a wider range of body types (Huffington Post 2012). Others are now focused on getting the same pledge from the editor of *Teen Vogue*, who to date has been far less receptive.[7] It would be misguided and inaccurate to claim that all young people feel this way or that social media is only used for political messaging; nevertheless, the examples above do challenge the suppositions forwarded by McRobbie and others who assert that dissent is dead or dying.[8]

A close reading of the sexualization literature shows that the enactment of corrupted or phallic femininity supersedes issues of representation and gender stereotypes in the media. Placing the extremity of claims (in terms of behavior and pathological outcomes) against the complex empirical and media landscape within which they are situated further illuminates this schism. The manner in which seemingly paradoxical feeling states such as protection, care, disgust, and anger are directed toward girls within this discourse signals that something far more complicated is at work. The girl described in the sexualization literature is not a girl in the messy material sense, but rather a symbol (the girl) forwarded in the service of something far greater. It is my contention that analyzing the deployment of sexuality, gender, and race within the sexualization literature will highlight several latent or unspoken registers of ambivalence that get pieced together in the composition of the sexualized girl.

Hyper-Heterosexualized Girlhood

Sexualizing materials catalyze hyper-heterosexuality. The sexualized girl's compulsive escapades defy, to the point of rupture, dominant conceptions of heterosexual femininity. Ironically, however, she is also excessively passive in her consumption (in that reception is always already uniform) and in her feminine acquiescence to male desire (she does whatever he pleases). She exemplifies a crisis in heterosexual femininity – wherein patriarchal visions of femininity no longer hold their value, but neither do feminist visions of gender. The repulsion underpinning this metamorphosis is transparent in conservative narratives which foreground lack of respectability, sexual aggressiveness, and a loss of modesty; and is evidenced in popular feminist texts which express distress and antipathy over the rise of self-objectification and self-sexualization. The sexualized girl is both hyper-feminine in her barely there mini-skirts and hyper-masculine in her misogynistic desire for objectification and the sex industry; as such, she falls far afield from acceptable constructions of feminist femininity and family values.

The conflation of sexualized girlhood with patriarchal masculinity sheds light on the pseudo-essentialist foundation upon which this discourse rests.[9] If sexualization has the capacity to change states of being – by turning children into adults and femininity into patriarchal masculinity – then it *de facto* changes states of nature. Quite simply, normal girls do not (cannot?) act the way sexualized girls do. A girl's sexuality is conceptualized as quiescent and inert, but also deeply fragile and, once stimulated, prone to perversion; in contrast, masculine heterosexuality is present, active, and natural. Although the female tween is constructed as passive and innocent, the propensity for corruption also speaks to an unacknowledged fear of inherent deviance, danger, and a need for control. The bifurcation of "sexual nature" is nothing new; it has been used to legitimate the social regulation of female eroticism as well as excuse the sexual violence of men in the Anglophone West since the nineteenth century (Hawkes 2004; Weeks 2009; Jackson and Scott 2010). Declarations of asexual innocence and wanton destruction were common constructions in the history of ideas on women's sexuality and more often than not were applied in an uneven fashion – heterosexual, white, middle-class, married women were more likely to be described as normal, chaste, and innocent before marriage, whereas women who were poor, of color, or lesbian got classified as promiscuous, dangerous, and in need of social regulation (Hawkes 2004). These restrictive gender and sexual ideologies continue to spur slut shaming and other forms of sexual bullying against girls perceived to be too desirous or too sexual (White 2004; Renold and Ringrose 2008, 2011). They are also at work in much of the popular literature on sexualization.

In discussions of pathological deficits, activities and modes of subjectivity, one quickly learns that hyper-heterosexualized girlhood is where the most sexist aspects of patriarchal capitalism come to see their own reflection. The girl is so responsive that even the slightest influence can produce a cataclysmic and uncontrollable outcome. Sexualized behaviors emerge from the masculine imaginary (which defines sexy) and are in service of the heterosexual male desire. As a sexual object, she seeks his gaze; in action, she is only attracted to boys her age or men far older; and finally, her desire is always already tethered to the male because it is his pleasure, not hers, which drives her actions. The sexualized girl is coterminously too feminine, too phallic, and too heterosexually active. Located at the intersection of hyper-reception and hyperactivity, the sexualized girl embodies the worst of both.

When sexualization is said to cause same-sex eroticism (e.g., two girls kissing), this action is viewed as a pornographic display used to titillate a male viewer (Oppliger 2008; M. Hamilton 2009a). Object identification – the desire to be with the figure on the screen as opposed to wanting to be like the figure on the screen – is rendered impossible within this discourse. Any type of ambivalence is ignored. But what if a girl wants to be with the female star and like her; conversely, what if she wants to be with the girl in the magazine precisely because she is so different? What if she wants to be like the girl some of the time, but not all of the time? None of these variations is possible because consumption can only encompass emulation and deviant transformation. Girls do not seek out, and seemingly cannot seek out, the female gaze, search for female sexual partners, or identify with queer women in popular culture (Gill 2009). Because sexualization is equated with hyper-heterosexualization, the possibility that queer girls could be sexualized or suffer its consequences is nowhere within the literature. Although this could be conceptualized positively – women never objectify girls and queer girls are immune from

Figure 2.2 Book covers from Gigi Durham (2008) and Maggie Hamilton (2009) offer a particularly illustrative example of the assumptions made within the literature. The white girls in Hamilton's cover are partially dressed (short skirts and belly shirts with high heels) and consumed with something or someone on the telephone. The girl on Durham's cover is equally salacious with eyes made up and mouth wide open. While it is interesting to note that both deploy sexualized images to sell their critiques of the same process, I am more interested in how the covers reflect a kind of visual semiotics of sexualization, which in the literature revolve around corrupted and pathologized white femininity. Of all the books reviewed in this book, only one features a young girl of color, Tanith Carey's *Where has My Little Girl Gone* (2011). Like the covers analyzed above, the girls on Carey's cover also gaze into an unseen mirror and seem all consumed with make-up. Girls are represented as self-absorbed and deeply narcissistic.

Sources: Gerald Duckworth & Co; Viking; Lion Hudson

sexualization – the essentialist tenets upon which the first assumption rests are dubious at best. Framing it another way, one might argue that since girls are naturally asexual at this age, sexual identity is irrelevant. Reading the claims regarding sexual behavior and self-objectification within this discourse, it becomes clear rather quickly that this explanation is equally illogical. The omission of queer sexuality speaks to the heteronormative presumption in the literature on sexualization, far more than a celebratory stance of queer resistance (Gill 2009). Reviewing how boyhood is conceptualized within the popular literature further illuminates the narrow lens within which gender and sexuality are framed.

Boys on the Side?

In *What's Happening to Our Boys?*, Maggie Hamilton describes the most pressing dangers facing "our" boys today (Hamilton 2011). Unlike her earlier work, *What's Happening to Our Girls?*, which chronicles how sexualizing culture stimulates promiscuous sexual action, mental and cognitive deficits, as well as a bleak future (in the sex industry, depressed, and alone), boys, it seems, are almost immune or, at the very least, far less affected (M. Hamilton 2009b, 2011). Although advertising directed toward boys may be predatory, in terms of creating loyal customers, its effects are far more benign; creating a desire for "coolness," "getting a girlfriend," or "acting like the older boys" (Hamilton 2011: 64). Readers are not privy to what any of this means because the risks are either self-evident or not particularly noteworthy (Hamilton 2011). One may surmise that sexualization is less likely because the (hetero)sexual subjectivity of boys is presumed to be both present and active (as opposed to present and absent); for example, self-objectification, self-sexualization as well as an interest in sex industry participation are nowhere mentioned. However, damage can occur after viewing graphic sexually explicit materials such as pornography, but its effects stimulate predation rather than promiscuity (Hamilton 2011). Bryan Duke, a father, states that consuming pornography is akin to "sexual abuse" because it awakens a boy's sexuality too soon (Duke, quoted in Hamilton 2011: 69). Interestingly, sexual awakening is not a longing for sexual exhibitionism (as it is for girls), but rather the craving for objectification and sexual violence. Like Hamilton, Diane Levin contends that pornography produces compassion deficit disorder (CDC) in boys and makes them more prone to sexual violence (Levin 2008). Given these distinctions, one must presume that male sexuality is inherently active and always already on the cusp of becoming out of control.

Hamilton and Levin both draw on the hypodermic model of reception – watching pornography creates pornographic subjectivity and sexuality. The rhetorical style and causal logic obscure good research on the complexity of boys and sexuality (McInnes 2004; Rasmussen 2004; Allen 2005; Pascoe 2007; McInnes and Davies 2008). This is not to say that pornography does not matter. Findings have shown that pornography fosters a patriarchal sense of hyper-masculinity in some boys (Pascoe 2007; Garlick 2010). It also makes some boys more likely to believe rape myths (women who are dressed a particular way are asking for it) and feel less empathy for rape victims (Coy et al. 2011). Porn consumption and pornographic talk are often used as a marker of masculinity and heterosexuality in groups and as a weapon to deride gay youth in high school (Pascoe 2007; Garlick 2010; Coy et al. 2011). However, that is not always the case and, equally important, not all pornography should be classified as violent and/or patriarchal (Attwood and Smith 2011). By ignoring the complexity of consumption, the sexual subjectivity of boys gets reduced to a patriarchal pornographic enactment. As a result, critical interrogation into the impact of a lack of positive sex education for straight, gay, bi, and trans boys, the confusion some boys feel about the differences between pornographic representation and *in vivo* sex, and the nuanced ways in which young men make meaning of pornography, are all questions that become marginal, at best, within the literature (Attwood and Smith 2011; Welsh Government 2011).

Sexual violence should not be treated lightly and clearly it is the responsibility of men to stop rape culture. Nevertheless, critical sexuality scholars should be wary of limiting causality and the sexuality of boys in this manner. The bodies of women and girls have long been ground zero for the reaffirmation of patriarchal masculinity, regulatory authority, and/or military might (to name just a few) through violence, sexual and otherwise, in the Anglophone West.[10] For this reason, a multi-causal model of violence against women is far more accurate and useful politically and sociologically. Sexualized media consumption may be a variable, but it should not be conceptualized as a singular cause. Although not as common, it is also important to note that boys' bodies are also subject to sexual violence, which extends beyond the violence of becoming a sexual predator.[11] Why is the construction of sex and sexuality so different?

One reason may be that the "sexual impulse" of heterosexual boys is considered natural and thus not liable to corruption in the same way. Within the sexualization literature, boys pose a threat because they have cultivated a pornographic sensibility, not because they are objectified (Hamilton 2011).[12] Object status – defined as something passive to be gazed upon for the sexual titillation of the viewer – is gendered female and/or heterosexual. As such, boys can only want to be like the male subject on the screen and not want to be with him. Moreover, they must want to be with the woman and not like her. Identification is definitively heteronormative and hyper-masculine. Although the discourse on sexualization presumes that once ignited a girl will seek out her own objectification (e.g., in a life on the pole), a boy doing the same is simply inconceivable. A passive, victimized, or objectified heterosexual boy is anathema in our contemporary culture, unless it is subjected to the homoerotic or perceived homoerotic gaze or touch (Kincaid 1998; see also Stockton 2009; Edelman 2004).[13]

A recent report published by the British-based Family Lives organization, entitled *All of our Concern: Commercialisation, Sexualisation and Hypermasculinity*, offers a powerful counterexample to the works described above (Family Lives 2012). *All of our Concern* highlights the impact of restrictive gender stereotypes, pornography, and sexual violence in the lives of boys, and offers recommendations for addressing peer-on-peer sexual violence, sexual and gendered bullying, gender stereotyping, and homophobia. Although its locus of concern is similar to that of Hamilton and Levin, it differs in its use of tone, conceptualization, and empirical literature. Addressing gendered stereotypes and representation, the report states, "qualitative studies have uncovered dominant exaggerated models of (heterosexual) masculinity in both state and private schools that are anti-academic, limit educational roundedness and put the brakes on boys fulfilling their academic potential" because of "bullying" that is inspired by sexist and homophobic attitudes (Family Lives 2012: 9). Sexual violence is linked to media

and the perpetuation of hyper-masculine beliefs and positive cor-
relations with rape myths (e.g., women dressed provocatively
deserve to be raped) and the idea that violence is sexy (Family
Lives 2012: 16). Unlike hypodermic conceptions of media reception, the report foregrounds a multi-causal model (media does not
cause sexual violence) and foregrounds power in its conception of
sexual violence.

The report also highlights the importance of talking to boys
and girls about pornography (it does not presume all boys or girls
feel the same way about it), foregrounds the necessity for positive
sex education, and emphasizes media literacy (although I vehemently disagree with its call for Internet censorship). The Family
Lives report tackles systemic cultural and representational issues
without reducing them to deviance or pathology. It is clear that
sexism, sexual violence, restrictive gender roles, and homophobia
are the problem, rather than the sexual child. Unfortunately, this
is not the case in most of the other literature on sexualization
– which raises the specter that the popular discourse is about
something more than its stated goals. Tracing the gendered and
heteronormative assumptions within the literature unearths the
epistemological framing upon which the sexualized girl is built
within this discourse and in so doing offers a more transparent
understanding of her as a symbol. Unpacking how race is being
deployed will uncover another epistemological line of support
upon which the construction of the sexualized girl is built within
the literature.

Whiteness at Risk

Sexualization is most often conceptualized as a perverse enactment
of white heterosexual girlhood (Fine 1998; Walkerdine 1998;
Gill 2009; Renold and Ringrose 2011; Bragg 2012a; Ringrose
2013). Unlike discussions of gender and sexuality which are so
exaggerated that they become easier to decipher, race functions
more covertly – whiteness is presumed unless otherwise stipulated.

Within discussions of sexualization, African American girls are tokenized at best, and the experiences of Latina girls, Asian girls, Indigenous girls, and South Asian girls (other than as victims of trafficking) are absented entirely. For example, in the books which have chapters that deal with hip hop or African American girls, the term "race" is used in the title which informs the reader that race is singularly conceptualized. Since discussions of girls of color are often absent, these chapters seem additive, rather than integral to the analysis (Olfman 2009; Durham 2008; for an exception, see APA 2007). Although Rihanna has come to serve as an example of sexualized sexuality and thus a risky choice for consumption, she pales in comparison to discussions of Lindsay Lohan, Miley Cyrus, Britney Spears, Paris Hilton, and Snooki from the MTV reality show, *Jersey Shore* (Hymowitz 2002; Rush and La Nauze 2006a; Oppliger 2008; M. Hamilton 2009a, 2009b; Maines 2009; Reist 2009a). In Clive Hamilton's discussion of sexualization and how good is the new bad (as opposed to the excesses of sexualized sexuality), the Obama girls are lauded as examples of respectable girlhood; however, using the Obama girls is the exception rather than the rule (C. Hamilton 2009). Simply put, whiteness needs no qualification because it operates as an unspoken norm. This is a curious omission in the feminist narratives on sexualization, since there is a rich literature on issues of race, class, gender, and representation as well as an emphasis on viewing gender as an experience that is inextricably linked to issues of race, class, sexuality, nation, ability, and religion (hooks 1992; Mohanty 2003; Barnard 2008; Hill Collins 2008; Nash 2008a, 2008b). As numerous critical race scholars have noted, part of the privilege of whiteness is located in its ability to go unarticulated and be taken for granted as the norm (hooks 1992; Omi and Winant 1994; Fanon 2008). The privilege of presumption is evident within most sexualization narratives to the extent that whiteness is present everywhere, but is rarely articulated as such. Examining the covers of books, analyzing the stars discussed in narratives of peril, and reviewing the examples of both good girls and bad, illustrates that sexualization is a racially specific threat to white, middle-class, heterosexual girls. How should we make sense of this?

One might argue that the risk posed is so universal that race is irrelevant and needs no elaboration because all girls are endangered. Or, one might claim that only white heterosexual girls are susceptible to such corrupting influence due to some facet of character, psychosocial makeup, or biological predisposition. Reviewing the stated claims regarding the ubiquity and unrelenting nature of sexualizing influences, that nevertheless ignore the issue of race when discussing endangered and dangerous girls, raises the specter that the locus of concern is narrow rather than inclusive and renders the idea of predisposition untenable. My analysis of the dematerialized quality of the girl within this discourse illustrates that she is a reflection of the group that views itself as most endangered. She is the amalgamation of white middle-class disquiet and deep anxiety from the left and the right. Within the Anglophone West, whiteness has been sutured to sexual innocence, childhood, and to various manifestations of "the future" – of the race, nation, or family (Cross 2004; Kincaid 1998; Sanchez-Eppler 2005; Anderson 2006; Egan and Hawkes 2010; Bernstein 2011). Historian Robin Bernstein argues that throughout the nineteenth century "a busy cultural system" was produced which linked "innocence to whiteness through the body of the child" (Bernstein 2011: 6). Accordingly, the "white child's innocence" got transferred to "surrounding people and things, and that property made it politically viable" (Bernstein 2011: 6).[14] In this sense, the material culture of childhood was cast as both free from adult concerns in its innocence while also being saturated with dominant adult concerns and anxieties regarding race and racial difference.[15] Warwick Anderson and Hugh Cunningham have made similar claims about the United Kingdom and Australia (Anderson 2006; Cunningham 2006).

In previous research, Gail Hawkes and I found that the protection of virtue, moral turpitude, and innocence of white middle-class children was a central tenet of sexual protection movements in the Anglophone West between 1860 and 1920 (Egan and Hawkes 2010). Sexual innocence is often a simile for white childhood; however, its security is always under threat and in need of vigilant protection – particularly for those concerned with social reformation (Egan and Hawkes 2010; Faulkner 2010).

More generally, the white child's sexuality has often served as a metaphor for national purity as well as an incredibly potent catalyst for fury and uproar when violated (Egan and Hawkes 2010; Bernstein 2011). The ubiquity of threats posed in terms of cultural contamination (theater, comic books, the city streets, etc.) or individuals (the "invert" and later homosexual, the immigrant, corrupt companion, and pedophile) reveals that the innocence of the white child is anything but assured. Moreover, the protection of innocence more often has served as a signifier for much larger cultural transformations (Kincaid 1998; Egan and Hawkes 2010).[16]

The metaphorical nature of the white child's sexuality within the sexualization literature reveals a historical and epistemological affinity between the current movement and sexual reform endeavors of the past. By conceptualizing sexualization as a sexually predatory force (what some have gone as far as calling corporate pedophilia) which defiles and sullies the sexual innocence of white girls, the figure of the sexualized girl inspires a deeply visceral response (Rush and La Nauze 2006a, 2006b). However, the sentimentalization of the past has given way to rage, disgust, mourning, care, and anxiety, all of which take center stage in the sexualization literature. Nevertheless there is, to use Robin Bernstein's phrase, "a busy cultural system" at work within this discourse, wherein whiteness gets grafted onto the figure of the girl and transferred onto a much larger social situation thereby justifying the need for intervention (Bernstein 2011). For conservatives she represents the fall of the family and future and evokes nostalgia for the past. For some feminists, she is proof positive that feminism's work is far from over, and speaks to a different kind of nostalgia, for the movement's past.

It may be the case that many popular feminist authors are falling into the trap that white liberal feminists have long been criticized for – ignoring issues of race, class, and sexual orientation. It is my contention that the sexualized girl is also serving another, albeit unacknowledged, purpose within the literature. She may represent the dashed hope of middle-class white liberal feminism (girls embracing phallic femininity instead of feminist visions of gender and achievement) as well as a figure that helps resuscitate and grant public validity to a certain type of feminist politics in an increasingly hostile or anti-feminist context. Historically, sexual protection movements granted female advocates a legitimate place in a context otherwise closed to them – the public sphere (Luker 1998; Stoller 2002; Haggis 2003; Agustin 2007; Egan and Hawkes 2010). In their endeavors to save the colonized, the poor, the prostitute, and the wayward child, white middle-class women gained both credibility and access to an expanded social sphere. Sexual protection movements did address important issues of inequality and worked for sexual autonomy (such as a woman's right to say no to sex and have some autonomy in the home), but they were also compelled by normalizing tendencies, particularly toward those deemed other (Luker 1998; Haggis 2003; Swain et al. 2009; Egan and Hawkes 2010). Similarly, anti-sexualization advocates raise critically vital questions about sexist representation, the continuation of patriarchy, the sleazy practices of corporate capital and sexual violence – all issues which need attention and demand social change. Notwithstanding, it is the construction of the sexualized girl, as a symbol, that is both narrowly conceptualized and universally defiled which has fueled a veritable industry of lecture tours, newspaper articles, blogs, parenting manuals, and hyperbolic television appearances. All too often this construction ignores the complexity of girls in the service of its message, and it is for this reason that it gives me pause – *as a feminist scholar* of sexuality. Resuscitating feminist authority through the figure of the sexualized girl is where this movement skirts perilously close to previous protection movements. Avoiding this is made all the more difficult because the sexualized girl intersects with and draws affective charge from longstanding Anglophone preoccupations with the sexual innocence of the white child.

Defiled Innocence and the White Cultural Imaginary

Within the Anglophone cultural imaginary, there are few ideas as potent and affectively charged as the sexual defilement of white innocence (Cross 2004; Cunningham 2006; Sanchez-Eppler 2006; Egan and Hawkes 2010; Faulkner 2010). Anti-sexualization narratives from the left and the right draw on this historically persistent fixation. The veracity of this attachment can be seen most clearly in times of violation, as in the coverage of the JonBenet Ramsey case, a young upper-middle-class white girl killed in her family's home by an unknown assailant in 1996, and in the reporting on Madeleine McCann, the young British girl who was abducted from her parent's room in Portugal in 2007. Reviewing the media frenzy surrounding both cases (at the time of the crimes and since), as well as the numerous books, websites (some of mourning, some set up to collect clues regarding the crime, and still others which seem akin to fan sites), posters, and the celebrity involvement that has taken place since – one can see just how powerful our attachment is to the white girl child as an object of protection, identification, and as a site of collective mourning. One would be hard pressed to find a case that comes close to the media coverage, cultural fascination, or persistent fervor (in the Ramsey case it has been 16 years) for any young girl of color in a similar circumstance.

The Janus-face of our cultural horror regarding the defilement of seraphic innocence is our culture's unacknowledged erotic attachment to youthful white innocence. Feminist anti-sexualization authors rightly note that our culture reproduces, at an alarming rate, sexualizing images in advertisements and other modes of popular culture. However, as literary scholar James Kincaid notes, our culture also has an unacknowledged and disavowed erotic fascination with the white child's innocence (Kincaid 1998). Kincaid's study examines the period before the sexualization debates, where blonde hair, blue-eyed innocence enraptured the viewing public. In his discussion of child actors (e.g., Shirley Temple and Dakota Fanning, but we could extend this to the Olsen twins, Abigail Breslin and even the bête noir of many sexualization authors, Miley Cyrus, before her descent), Kincaid argues that our culture becomes definitively less attached when such figures hit adolescence, at which point they either leave the public eye until later or become sexual objects and often face social sanctions. According to Kincaid, we project our cultural fascination

Figure 2.3 The prolonged media attention sparked by the Madeleine McCann and JonBenet Ramsey cases render visible the extent to which our culture is both horrified by and attached to the violation of the white child's body. This is not to deny the horrific quality of these crimes, but rather to illustrate the popularity and potential for stories such as these to capture the anglophile imagination. It is noteworthy that in the popular press, child beauty pageants and sexualization came under fire with the JonBenet Ramsey case; however, it was her parents and the industry that was critiqued. Nowhere did JonBenet's participation translate into any kind of deficit on her part. Similarly, Madeleine McCann's mother was treated with particular insensitivity in the press. Nevertheless, the level of cultural attachment to these cases can be seen in the images above and in their persistence (e.g., the poster campaign to find Maddy was on buses, subways, and television shows, and was supported by celebrities such as David Beckham in the UK, and the JonBenet case has been featured four times on the cover of the very popular *People* magazine).

Source: People magazine (www.people.com)

with innocence onto the figure of the lurking pedophile, to the detriment of the fact that most sexual violence against children happens in the home or with friends of the family. Ironically, our fears of stranger danger and our vigilant desire to rid our streets of it allow the innocent child (and the child defiled if we think of television shows such as *Law and Order: SVU* and the numerous other police dramas which render the sullied child a spectacle) to remain firmly in view. Such spectacles and social anxieties help us disavow our attachment by recasting it as an issue of protection. This creates a cultural context where it "seems better to take a child's life" than her "virtue" (Kincaid 1998: 16). As Kincaid rightly questions, "if we teach ourselves to regard the loss of innocence as more calamitous than the loss of life . . . do we feel that a defiled child is of no use to us and might as well be dead?" (Kincaid 1998: 17).

The sexualized girl *affects us* because it draws on our longstanding cultural cathexis for the sexually innocent white child in both its angelic and defiled status. *I am not arguing that advocates from the right or the left are manipulatively using our cultural fears regarding the defilement of white sexual innocence to forward their claims.* Rather, I am pointing out that their concerns travel along the same affective chain of associations and thus have the potential to ignite a particular set of cultural ideas and feelings. If we revisit the metaphor of the armature (as the taken-for-granted epistemological and affective support structure upon which the production of the sexualized girl rests) discussed in the Introduction, we see that our cultural imaginary regarding gender, sexuality, and race is central to the construction of this frame. The sexualized girl sparks a powerful visceral response because it rests upon a larger and historically persistent fascination for the white child's sexual innocence. Uncovering this connection illuminates, at least in part, why a discourse like this might be taken up with more ease than another which grates against a deeply held object of cultural affection. However, it is important to remember that this is only part of the affective armature at work in this discourse.

Conclusion

The sexualized girl is a bloated symbol that speaks to numerous cultural purposes coterminously – for conservatives she serves as an emblem of the erosion of the patriarchal family, gender, and whiteness, and for feminism she is proof of a movement's decline as well as its hope for the future. Deconstructing the epistemological and affective frame upon which this symbol relies illuminates the socio-historical and affective lineage that come together in complementary and conflicted ways in the deployment of this discourse. Tracing the ways in which gender, race, and sexuality are deployed highlights how this figure draws on a host of seemingly paradoxical cultural anxieties (e.g., traditional family, the future of feminism, sexual innocence, sexual promiscuity, etc.) to become meaningful and affectively compelling.

The girl (in her sexualized and innocent state) is a site of condensation, wherein a variety of fears, anxieties, and wishes get tangled together and often go unchallenged. Ultimately she is a figure into which we project culture ambivalence, fear, disgust, and desire. It is only through tracing the various discursive and affective filaments that weave together in the creation of this symbol that we can begin to have a better understanding of her purpose. More metaphor and myth, the girl as a figure within sexualization narratives reflects a set of latent concerns regarding the social order and the future. In conservative narratives, once sexualized she functions as a symbol of cultural decline and as a portent of an endangered future. Her pre-sexualized (read innocent) or normalized counterpart signifies nostalgia and enables the redeployment of respectable femininity, heteronormativity, and a more stable future.

Conservative discourses on sexualization and its outcomes are a wish for a nostalgic return to a better time of faith, family, and patriarchal authority. The sexualized girl represents a nihilistic future that must be defended against, and as such she may inspire a nostalgic return to innocence, respectability, the unproblematic valorization of whiteness, and family values. Recent data from the Pew Charitable Trust shows that the face of marriage, at least in the United States, is rapidly changing (Cohn 2011; Wang 2012). Wendy Wang, a researcher for Pew, found that despite the fact that 43 percent of families stated that they would be "uncomfortable" with interracial marriage in their own family, interracial marriages have more than tripled in the past two decades (Wang 2012). D'vera Cohn has shown that new marriage rates are down and that "barely half" of American heterosexual adults are married (Cohn 2011). Moreover, the fight for marriage equality is being waged all over the United States and is already a reality in England and parts of Australia. Within this context, one can gain a sense of why conservatives are in a panic regarding the future of the heteronormative, patriarchal white family and how the sexualized girl functions as a cautionary tale. The nostalgia inherent in much of the conservative narratives on sexualization speaks to a desire to look backward in the hopes of holding onto a bucolic vision of times past – however, it is always helpful to remember that nostalgia more often than not functions as a fantasy for something that never really was. Or, at the very least, a vision of the past that was only "great" for a precious few. Nonetheless, the manner in which sexualization is conceptualized (as ubiquitous and akin to toxic air) may reveal just how fragile the fantasy of reviving the past actually is within the movement.

As I noted at the beginning of this chapter, the feminist authors under analysis are responding to a very material shift in popular culture and the landscape of representation. There is no doubt that corporations seem to thrive on the production of increasingly salacious spectacles of young female bodies in the service of profit making. In magazines and other media directed toward girls, we see a narrow "heterosexual address" and one that reproduces a painful, narrow vision of gender and sexuality (Jackson and Westrupp 2010). Most depressingly, we still live in a world where sexual harassment, sexual exploitation, sexual violence, and domestic abuse are far too common in the lives of women and girls. Within this context, I feel deep resonance with the frustration and the strong desire for change expressed by many authors in anti-sexualization texts. It is in the construction of the sexualized girl as a representation of white heteronormative girlhood as well as in the construction of the problem as one of pathology where I part company. Within the sexualization literature, the sexualized girl represents the forward march of patriarchical capital and proof of what has been lost, and finally why the fight is still necessary. In many popular feminist arguments, protecting girls from sexualization both resuscitates and validates anti-pornography arguments, thereby reinstalling its validity as the voice of protection in an otherwise "post-feminist" moment.

The girl in this discourse is so weighed down by adult need (for stability) and desire (for the future) that she functions primarily as an empty vessel into which the instabilities, anxieties, and desires of both the left and the right get placed. Through her defilement and corruption, we can express our rage and disgust, and ultimately through her normalization we can move toward the fantasy of a more stable future. She is evocative and compelling – but in the end, she is an imaginary figure that adults need because she allays our sense of impotence and fear. For this reason, she becomes a talisman or defense mechanism that we create to shield us from the intolerable insecurity that comes from living in what sociologist Stephen Pfohl calls the "ultra modern" world (Pfohl 1992). In the next chapter I will explore this claim through an analysis of social class and classism in the discourse on sexualization.

3

Sexualized Tastes, Middle-Class Fantasies, and Fears of Class Contagion

The commodification of women and girls is now so ingrained in our culture that glamour modeling and lap-dancing are widely viewed not only as acceptable but in some cases aspirational.

Linda Papadopoulos (2010), *Sexualization of Young People Review*

In our parents' and grandparents' time, little girls – at least those whose parents strove for middle-class respectability – were socialized to be modest, polite and obedient. In the 1930s, Shirley Temple was Fox Studios' most lucrative star; her innocent eyes wore no mascara, her giggle had no trace of campy irony, and she kept her fans happy without ever baring a nipple ring. Into the 1950s and early 1960s, fresh-faced little girls like her were the norm . . . Whatever happened to little girls?

Val Ross (2011), What happened to little girls? *ParentingCanada*

Of course, there have always been high-class prostitutes and courtesans: girls from respectable families who have chosen to lead unrespectable lives. But that's just the point. Respectable people considered their activities to be shameful.

Melanie Phillips (2010), How did the world's oldest profession become a career choice for middle-class girls?

Introduction

During the early autumn of 2010, British tabloids circulated a story of two young women, Jenny Thompson and Helen Wood, who while working as escorts secured funds from a famous footballer, Wayne Rooney, for a *ménage à trois*. This story was made all the more salacious because Rooney was not only married, but his pretty young wife was also, at the time, very pregnant. The emotional tenor of the coverage caught my eye, because star athletes paying for sex and women working in the sex industry are not particularly remarkable, and as we are often reminded in these kinds of stories, prostitution is "the oldest profession in the world." Nevertheless, the contempt and rage directed toward Thompson and Wood is almost palpable in the media. "Whoring," "sleazy," "vulgarity," "stupidity," "greedy," "deluded," "sickening," "raddled, used up and unwanted," "degrading," "turning themselves into objects" are a sample of the adjectives used to describe the women and their actions in the various blogs, opinion editorials, and news coverage of this story (Mooney 2010; Phillips 2010; Davies 2010). When reading the editorials surrounding this case, one begins to understand that prostitution per se is not a problem; rather, the derision, contempt, and "deep anger" expressed by authors is being induced by the transgression of another boundary, social class. The most remarkable aspect for most authors is that Thompson and Wood are "privately educated" girls from "respectable" families (Phillips 2010; Ross 2011). Worse still, in the photos displayed, they appear to be unashamed and unapologetic. When authors ask, "What have we come to when middle-class girls like this see whoring as a career choice?" or, "How did the world's oldest profession become a career choice for middle-class girls?" the class-coded nature of this call for repudiation becomes crystal clear (Mooney 2010; Phillips 2010). Reaction toward Rooney, the one who paid Wood and Thompson and cheated on his then pregnant wife, is not warm but it is decidedly less vitriolic – he is represented as a "rough, over-paid, self-indulgent fool" and just one among many of his equally feckless peers (Mad Dog and Glory 2010; Mooney 2010).

When respectable middle-class girls go bad, it is "something different; something very, very troubling," and for this reason it spurs a particularly intense affective response (Mooney 2010; Carey 2011). Commentators express that Wood and Thompson deserve an unhappy and desperate life because, "their behaviors pollute the lives of younger girls they will never meet – by setting a terrible example" (Mooney 2010). Wood and Thompson not only violated middle-class standards of acceptable sexual practice, they did so flagrantly and with abandon and as a result they aroused anger, disgust, and embarrassment (Mooney 2010). This breech spurs strong visceral reactions which have their roots in middle-class fantasies regarding the tastes and practices of the working class which have a long history in the Anglophone West. Melanie Phillips' comments echo these sentiments when she states that high-end prostitution has been around for a very long time, but unlike Wood and Thompson, those women "considered their activities shameful" (Phillips 2010). The popular website, caughtoffside.com, expressed a similar cultural conception, "Suffice to say these women are pretty much the bottom of a very dirty barrel. These 'occasional' prostitutes have decided that the best way to get ahead (no pun intended) is to sleep with people for money and then sell their stories to the press" (Mad Dog and Glory 2010). Given their actions, Wood and Thompson deserve whatever bad luck, unhappiness, or even violence, to befall them.

The consequences of such behavior were further evidenced in recent reporting on two different events that took place over the summer of 2011. The first involved Ms. Thompson being chased out of a pub by a crowd of angry women who were said to be "friends of Coleen Rooney" (the wife of Wayne) in Liverpool, and the second happened two months later – when Ms. Wood was kicked and beaten by a "baying mob" chanting Rooney's name in a Manchester pub (Daily Mail Reporter 2011). In this story, and in far too many to chronicle since, both women are referred to as "Wayne Rooney vice girl," "Wayne Rooney's hooker." The story of Ms. Wood's public beating in the *Daily Mail* began with "the prostitute who slept with Wayne Rooney while his wife was pregnant . . ." (Daily Mail Reporter 2011). It seems that these women have been branded with a kind of postmodern scarlet letter and once marked always shamed. At base, they are viewed as tainted, monstrous, and deserving of public shaming and, it seems, even beating.

Why bring up the representations of Wood and Thompson in my analysis of the discourse on sexualization of girls? Although at first glance this case seems to substantiate the arguments of many anti-sexualization advocates (sexualization catalyzes an almost pre-ternatural desire for the sex industry), I posit it also grants ingress into a central, albeit often implicit, assumption about social class at work within cultural narratives on the topic. The affective quality of the coverage of Wood and Thompson and the language used is not dissimilar to discussions of sexualized girlhood. It is my con-tention that the thread which connects the two is an affective one; both are inspired by and reproduce feelings of anger, disgust, and anxiety which are induced by middle-class female bodies being tainted and transformed into something horrific – a bawdy work-ing-class female who refuses the norms of "respectable femininity" and middle-class sexual decorum, an outcome which Thompson and Wood seem to represent.

Such presumptions reflect longstanding middle-class anxieties that are part and parcel of dominant Anglophone cultural fantasies, projec-tions, and ideological formations about the eroticism, bodily comportment, and taste of the poor and working class. Constructing the working class, poor, colonial, and non-white immigrant as more bodily, bawdy, erotic, and wanton has a long history in the Anglophone cultural imaginary (Stallybrass and White 1986; Bourdieu 1987; McClintock 1995; Stoller 1995, 2002; Elias 1996; Walkerdine 1998). In this regard, the discourse on sexualization bears the mark of Anglophone middle- and upper-middle-class fixations expressed since the eighteenth century (Foucault 1980; Stallybrass and White 1986; Hunt 1999; Mort 2000; Anderson 2006; Egan and Hawkes 2010). Middle-class perceptions and/or fantasies regarding the poor have been taken for granted as truthful and have underpinned social movements (social purity, hygiene, and eugenics), disciplines (hygiene, medicine, criminology, sociology, and psychology), and institutions (public health and social work) which sought to regulate and normalize the erotic practices of the working class, the poor, the immigrant, or the colonized (Foucault 1980; Mort 2000; Anderson 2006; Egan and Hawkes 2010). Historian Gary Cross illustrates the persistence of such ideas when he states, sexualized forms of dress and behavior "from working-class or minority neighborhoods" have long been assumed to be a primary characteristic of poor families and these presumptions have been used to legitimate racist and classist projections of poor parents as inept and unable "to protect their children from evil" (Cross 2004: 11; see also Sanchez-Eppler 2005). Against this, the white bourgeois body has been conceptualized as pure, hygienic, and emblematic of restraint and rationality; and the middle- and upper-class child the embodiment of innocence, purity, and the bright future of the class, race, and nation (Walkerdine 1998; Anderson 2006; Egan and Hawkes 2010).

Taste and comportment within this equation are metonymically linked to both class membership and gender presentation (e.g., working class + female = sexually promiscuous). Moreover, working-class taste in terms of clothes, manners, and bodily practice are always already assumed to be low, overly erotic, and unrestrained (Stallybrass and White 1986). When demarcations of taste and comportment become porous, the boundaries of class, gender, and in the case of sexualization, childhood itself seem permeable at best and ruptured at worst (working class = loss of innocence = loss of childhood + girl = destined to be promiscuous = future in ruins). This may explain why current anxieties expressed in sexualization narratives which point toward the danger of one's daughter becoming a "girl from the other side of the tracks" produce such an evocative response.

Unpacking how adults read girls in terms of motivations, desire, and the future, through their taste in objects, is a crucial question in discussions of sexualization. Although the sexist nature of the patriarchal gaze in dominant media has received ample consideration in the literature, the gaze of the critic has gone unchallenged (APA 2007; Rush and La Nauze 2006a; Durham 2008; Papadopoulos 2010; Carey 2011; Dines 2011). Remedying this absence by unpacking how the complexity of history, gender, class, and sexuality can produce affective responses that may unwittingly shape perceptions and proclamations about girls and their future seems particularly important. Situating the discourse on sexualization within a larger socio-historical landscape reveals how historically trenchant fears of class contagion (which are fueled by deeply problematic projections of the other) are embedded in much of the literature on sexualization. By analyzing class-coded assumptions regarding class, sexuality, and gender, one can see that, for many authors, the threat posed by sexualization is the erosion of middle-class respectability and the transformation of good middle-class girls into their working-class poor counterparts. Nevertheless, it is important to restate that this anxiety is based upon a set of middle-class presumptions about the eroticism of the poor, and as such it is not an accurate reflection of the lives of girls who are poor or middle-class.

Taste and the Middle-Class Imaginary

Manners and taste are cultural phenomena through which class distinctions get encoded and reproduced (Bourdieu 1987). Taste, then, is never simply about personal affinity; rather, it is about entering into a cultural system, whereby objects reflect corporate, cultural, and socio-historical coding (in the dominant and potentially subversive sense of the term) (Bourdieu 1987; Levine 1990; Gronow 1997; Gans 1999; Brottman 2005).[1] However, the ways in which an object "speaks" is neither singular nor automatic, and is often a site of contestation. Qualifiers and descriptions such as "good," "bad," "trashy," or "tasteful" are not reflective of some irrefutable essence of an object – they are cultural designations. Aesthetic judgments are the result of history (individual and social), culture, capitalism, and media, and may also reflect a vested interest in the reproduction of a particular system of social class, religion, or gender (to name only a few) (Bourdieu 1987). Within this dense and deeply nuanced constellation of culture, history, and biography, I want to focus on the ways in which social class and gender are read and contested through taste and manners. More specifically, I am interested in how designations of class difference are produced and reaffirmed by the standards of middle- and upper-middle-class taste as well as what happens when these boundaries become fluid or perceived as such.

Analyzing treatises on manners and cultural instruction (on everything from nose blowing to where one should sleep and what one should wear to bed), historian Norbert Elias illustrates how the inculcation of manners and bodily practices reflects larger socio-historical shifts and the reinforcement of social class divisions from the fifteenth century onward in Europe (Elias 1996). Distinctions in practices such as eating, dress, and comportment operate as if inspired by nature because of the ways in which affect gets grafted onto them (Elias 1996: 103). Mobilizing affect naturalizes societal dictates by erecting thresholds of shame and disgust which police the boundaries of acceptable and unacceptable displays of dress, comportment, and manners. Elias' case studies (e.g., from eating with one's hands from a common bowl to the use of separate plates and the use of utensils) elucidate how "the embodiment of a specific standard of emotions and a specific level of revulsion . . . [speak to] a change in the structure of drives and emotions" regarding particular practices (1996: 103). Designations of shame or disgust are not natural, but are "molded according to a social structure" (1996: 113). As "the social reference of shame and embarrassment recedes more and more from consciousness" and comes to operate "with regard to everyone and is imprinted in this form on the child, it seems to the adult a command of his own inner self and takes on the form of a more or less total and automatic self-restraint" (1996: 114). Taste and manners install a kind of cultural superego and boundary between bourgeois bodily practices and what was historically considered the bawdy, untoward, and unkempt practices of the poor, the insane, and later, I would add, the colonized. As a result, "the circle of precepts and regulations is tightly drawn" and seems to offer only two solutions: "submit" or "be excluded from life in decent society" (1996: 116). While what gets classified within these designations shifts over time and varies according to culture, what Elias powerfully illustrates is how they function as regulatory devices made palpable by affect.

Drawing on the work of Norbert Elias, French sociologist Pierre Bourdieu argues that cultural dictates on manners and taste function as one of the most powerful tools in the reproduction of social class (Bourdieu 1977). As Bourdieu states, if every society that attempts to

> produce a new man through a process of deculturation and recultura-
> tion set such store on the seemingly most insignificant details of dress,
> bearing, physical and verbal manners, the reason is that, treating the
> body as a memory, they entrust to it in abbreviated and practice, i.e.,
> mnemonic, form the fundamental principles of the arbitrary content of
> the culture. These principles embodied in this way are placed beyond
> the grasp of consciousness, and hence cannot be touched by volun-
> tary, deliberate transformation . . . [the] trick of pedagogic reason lies
> precisely in the way it extorts the essential while seeming to demand
> the insignificant . . . the concessions of *politeness* always contain *political*
> concessions (Bourdieu 1977: 94–5).

For Bourdieu, the pedagogy of taste (vis-à-vis clothing, manners, and comportment) creates a deep, and often unconscious, structure of class reproduction for members of every social class. This peda-gogy is central to the way in which taste functions as a symbolic marker of habitus – the dispositions and practices of a particular class status (Bourdieu 1987). Dominant conceptions of good taste bare the mark of the socio-political and thus rely upon and per-petuate a particularly classed conception (or projection) of gender, race, age, and sexuality (Bourdieu 1987; Elias 1996; Douglas 2002). It also sheds light on why violations of taste and "polite-ness" may trigger an emotional response. Guardianship over the "proper" and respectable can be fierce and, when breeched, often inspires a powerful response ranging from disgust and embar-rassment to outrage and, at times, desire. The boundaries of the culturally acceptable, normal, or class appropriate are secured by the bricks and mortar of affect and social sanction.

The affective nature of transgression makes the deconstruction of taste far more difficult; nevertheless, both Bourdieu and Elias highlight that this response is a *social* phenomenon, one that is linked to the production of difference and inequality. The social quality of this endeavor becomes more transparent when examining the lengths to which adults will go to instill such practices in their children. However, because social designations regarding class and taste are the product of culture, they are far from monolithic – as such, it is important to remember that boundary crossing has a long history in the Anglophone West and brings with it both erotic excitement and fears of social disintegration. The borders demarcating class and taste become far more affectively charged and vigilantly defined when they are, or are perceived to be, blurred and porous. Regulation is nothing new, but analyzing its operation reveals persistent anxieties about the fragile nature of middle-class sensibility, practice, and desire. In this sense the desire for transgression, as well as the necessity for regulation and normalization, seem to go hand in hand. However, the freedom to transgress and/or the compulsion to police have often had a particularly gendered quality.

A striking example of this can be found in cultural, usually patriarchal, fantasies of transforming the "uncouth" or "crass" working-class woman into a woman of society as represented in *Pygmalion* or its various adaptations in films such as *My Fair Lady, Educating Rita, Pretty Woman*, or the far tamer Disney versions, *Cinderella* or *The Prince and Me*. The eroticism and delight of border crossing and the desire to, in bell hooks' words, "taste a bit of the other" is another variant on this fantasy and has been featured in an untold number of films and novels (hooks 1992). Nevertheless, it is another kind of recurrent middle-class boundary work one sees in the sexualization literature – the desire to police the borders of middle-class comportment and sexual respectability through moral and/or political means.

Since the late nineteenth century, risk to children has often been conceptualized as emerging from the environmental, moral, and/ or genetic deficiencies of the poor, working class, or the sexually "deviant" (Gordon 1999; Mort 2000; Sanchez-Eppler 2005; Egan and Hawkes 2008). Historically, middle-class and upper-class women were considered well suited and, in some cases, more legitimate voices in advocating for moral behavior, sexual respectability, provision of sex education, and child rearing. Because these issues spoke to and reaffirmed dominant conceptions of femininity, women could engage in public discourse and action while avoiding social sanction for violating gender norms. The goals of these movements were complex and ranged from the progressive (e.g., purity activists wanted women to have more freedom in marital relations and temperance activists were actively fighting against issues of male violence) to the regulatory and normalizing (Hunt 1999; Mort 2000; Haggis 2003; Anderson 2006; Egan and Hawkes 2010). Although instruction on taste, behavior, and child rearing did include men,[2] middle-class women were central in crafting the vision, goals, and agenda for social change in movements which sought to protect both children and women from sex (Luker 1989; Hunt 1999; Mort 2000; Hall 2004; Egan and Hawkes 2007, 2010).

My research with Gail Hawkes revealed how these assumptions were foundational to the child-rearing materials created by social purity activists as well as the sexual and social hygiene manuals and pamphlets published in the early 1900s (Egan and Hawkes 2007, 2010). The poor were considered particularly perilous, even infectious, because their everyday practices were believed to violate "the boundaries of the civilized body" and as such "the boundaries which separated the human from the animal" (Stallybrass and White 1986: 132). Consequently, working-class pleasures and practices (e.g., bawdy theaters, loud music, dancing, fairs, and ale houses) were thought to be the greatest threat to childhood innocence and the formation of a more civilized society (Stallybrass and White 1986; Hunt 1999; Mort 2000; Egan and Hawkes 2007, 2010). Without sustained intervention in the tenets of social purity, activists believed that middle-class children would be drawn into a life of masturbation and later degeneracy (Stallybrass and White 1986; Mort 2000; Egan and Hawkes 2007, 2010).

Hindering class and race contamination through the instillation of monogamy and middle-class values was a central platform for the sexual hygiene movement in the Anglophone West (Egan and Hawkes 2010). Hygienists attempted to redirect the gender and

Figure 3.1 This poster from the American Social Hygiene Commission
was created for the Army to instill a sense of responsibility in their
young recruits. Although they wanted to shock viewers with such
images, they also sought to instill a sense of the future in men who
might otherwise seek out sexual liaisons with a dangerous (read, poor)
woman in the sex trade. In contrast, the home and hearth get
represented by the wife and children in an idyllic space, and are coded
with middle-class sensibilities. A key pedagogical tenet of the hygiene
movement in the Anglophone West was the instillation of middle-class
values of monogamy and gender into the working-class child (Egan and
Hawkes 2010).

Source: University of Minnesota Library Social Welfare Archive

sexual predilections of the working class through the habituation
and correct (sex) instruction of children, in the hopes of curbing
dysgenics to create a more "civilized" and "fit" society (Egan
and Hawkes 2010). As reformer M.E. Robinson claimed, good
instruction in social and sexual hygiene "will eventually make

[laws restricting marriage among the unfit] unnecessary and bring about the perfect adaptation of sex desire and even, perhaps, of sexual power and fertility, to the social need for the renewal of the population" (Robinson 1911: 339). Like earlier movements, I argue that the discourse on sexualization is plagued by an enduring middle-class fantasy of the poor and its seemingly corrupting quality. Although the problem differs (urban working-class displays versus popular culture), the sexualization literature, like purity and sexual hygiene before it, relies upon and reproduces a conception of the working poor as other and is sustained by fears of class contagion. What is strikingly different is that, in the current movement, only girls seem to be at risk (Egan and Hawkes 2007, 2008, 2010; Renold and Ringrose 2011; Ringrose 2011). The Pygmalion fantasy and the fantasy of class contamination share a particular set of assumptions about the erotic quality of women and girls from the wrong side of the social class divide. Both revolve around the tension produced between the registers of "desire/contamination" (Stallybrass and White 1986: 136). This is particularly evident in discussions of clothing, comportment, and in the use of the word "skank."

The "Fine Hemline Between Stylish and 'Skanky'"

In *Girls Gone Skank: The Sexualization of Girls in American Culture*, Patrice Oppliger forwards a common argument found in popular treatises on sexualization, that the consumption of sexualized products stimulates sexual action (Oppliger 2008). Popular culture and the behavior it produces in girls have hit a new low and this cultural condition, according to Oppliger, will not be changing any time soon. Her analysis of youth culture focuses specifically on clothing and how fashion has devolved from "sexy to slutty to skanky" over the last two decades (Oppliger 2008). Elucidating the term for the uninformed, Oppliger states that "skank chic is also known as 'trailer park fashion' or 'dumpster chic'" (Oppliger 2008: 9). In a chapter-long treatment of "common skank features," she describes the rise and fall of the thong (and whale tail), the ubiquity of low-rise jeans and other clothing items which draw attention to the "crotches," "breasts," and/or "rear cleavage" of young teen and tweenaged girls (Oppliger 2008: 10). She claims that "the most skanky colors are white and pink, which is ironic because they generally signify purity and femininity . . . [however,] these colors are generally more revealing, so that others can see darker colored underwear and bra underneath" (Oppliger 2008: 10).

Donning salacious and sexualized clothing, exhibitionistic girls seek out excitement in school yards, dances, and at the mall. In a subsection of the same chapter, entitled "Prostitots" (defined as "little girls who are dressed like adult women in the sex trade"), the reader is informed that "skank wear" is not just for teens, but is also being marketed and consumed by children as young as five (Oppliger 2008: 15). Oppliger's concerns echo the laments expressed by conservative columnists who critique the rise of "skankily-clad kids" at Halloween with questions such as, is "your kindergartner trick-or-treating in a bumblebee outfit a prostitute might wear?" (Raezler 2008; Fyfe 2008). As Colleen Raezler, columnist for the *Media and Culture Institute*, states, formerly creative Halloween attire is "being replaced by skimpy costumes more appropriate for brothels" and marketed to girls as young as five (Raezler 2008). Clothing choice becomes synonymous with "raunchy behavior" and by implication a girl's future (Hill 2010).

In her recent piece for the *Wall Street Journal*, Jennifer Moses asserts that although many in her generation chose not to worry about issues of "reputation" or waiting for sex until marriage when they were young, they find themselves ashamed and embarrassed when they look back on their youthful indiscretions (Moses 2011).[3] Further underscoring her point, Moses asserts that she has never met a woman who "wishes she'd [sexually] experimented more" when she was a girl (Moses 2011). As such, Moses is befuddled as to why so many mothers can feel shame about their own past, and yet continue to let their daughters "dress like prostitutes," particularly when the risks facing girls today are exponentially greater (Moses 2011). According to Moses, standing idly by is like telling your tweenaged daughter, "for heaven's sake, get laid!"

Figure 3.2 Book covers from Levin and Kilbourne (2008), Oppliger (2008), and Flanagan (2011) highlight both the logic and classist imagination at work in the sexualization literature. The white body is displayed as uncovered or unzipped and ready to become the eroticized figure on display. In each, the visual image is meant to affect the reader – it is the transformation of white youth into something crass or wanton that is at stake and thus should inspire the reader to take action.

Sources: Ballantine Books; McFarland & Co; Reagan Arthur

(Moses 2011).[4] Clothes and comportment matter, and without surveillance and intervention mothers may, albeit unknowingly, promote promiscuity now and deep regret in the future.

Within the sexualization literature, clothing functions in a metonymic fashion whereby it gets equated with action and later subjectivity (thong = sexualized action = sexualized girlhood). As a result, "skanky" items come to signify or predict a girl's descent down the slippery slope toward sexualized activities. Middle-class cultural fantasies regarding the working-class child have long assumed its erotic quality (the result of bad parenting or genetics). This production of difference is constitutive in that its depravity is used as the category against which middle-class, and most often white, innocence gets constructed as well as a justification for normalizing intervention from outside institutions (Walkerdine 1998; Sanchez-Eppler 2005; Anderson 2006; Egan and Hawkes 2010; Faulkner 2010). At base, innocence cannot work without its working-class counterpart. If we take this into account, the metonymic chain becomes more complicated because clothing is linked to action and the transformation of middle-class girlhood into the fantasy of the working-class other (e.g., clothing (associated with working class) = action = a working-class subjectivity). This fantasy is rendered visible in the adjective "skanky" and its conceptualization as both a catalyst and an outcome. This logic is also at work when authors caution readers about the "trickle down" effects of sexualization (Bray 2008, 2009; Rush 2009; Papadopoulos 2010). Within this logic, tawdry T-shirts, undergarments, and Halloween costumes come to operate as both an aesthetic violation and a predictive medium (APA 2007; Oppliger 2008; Walter 2010; Carey 2011).

Projection and the Other

Projection often feels akin to prescience because of the way in which affect colors our understanding; it is a fantasy formation about the other that *feels* completely self-evident. On one level, it functions as a mechanism whereby the individual rids her- or himself of unwanted feelings or disavowed desires by projecting them onto the other. In so doing, what one loathes about oneself transforms into the danger posed by the other. To some extent then, projection works like an inversion of the American children's phrase "I'm rubber you're glue, whatever you say bounces off me and sticks to you;" which is transformed into "I am rubber and you are glue, whatever I don't like about myself bounces off me and sticks to you." It is crucial to remember that projection is not simply the province of individuals. Projections, particularly in the service of dominant ideals, are imbued with power and legitimacy and have, at times, dangerous outcomes. A dominant cultural imaginary informs, along with a host of other complex variables, cultural conceptions of national identity, national culture, and validates particular actions (war or crafting of immigration policies) by tinting our perceptions of the other. Cultural conceptions of acceptable manners, tastes, eroticism, or lack thereof, are re-instantiated and reaffirmed by projecting our desire or revulsion onto other cultures or individuals.[5] Attending to the language and affective tenor of the discourse on sexualization reveals how taste, class, gender, and comportment are read through the distorting lens of projection. The way we read the other and the assumptions we project onto them may or may not (or may a little, but not completely) illuminate at all how an individual identifies (and thus also engages in fantasy) with the various messages and meanings of what or how she or he is wearing a particular item.

In much of the literature on sexualization, the problem does not stop at clothing choice, but extends to the types of bodies wearing inappropriate clothing. For example, Oppliger comments that "a skank look is also created when clothes fit too tightly" (e.g., wearing a pair of pants that are a size too small) to "create a muffin top" (Oppliger 2008: 11). Sexualized or "skanky" transgressions extend beyond fleshy (young) bodies to include "older women [who] dress too young" (Oppliger 2008: 11). When "flesh spills out" of the clothes worn by young girls, or older women "expose stretch marks, leathery patches of skin from sun overexposure and varicose veins," an offense has taken place, but exactly what and who is injured in this logic – the sexualized or the spectator? The construction of harm gets knotty because content (what is on the T-shirt, thong, etc.), condition (the types of clothes, but in equal measure the unfit bodies in them), and causation (what said clothing incites) get conflated as sexualization; nevertheless, this conceptual collapse points toward longstanding middle-class revulsion toward and desire for the bawdy bodily displays of the working class, and endeavors to reinforce the boundaries of middle-class taste and respectability.

Oppliger's descriptions find common cause with fashion editor Justine Cullen's (2011) recent comments in an editorial for Australian magazine *Shop Til You Drop* on "socially acceptable slut-tiness" (Cullen, quoted at 30isthenewblack.com). We are told that women and girls should not worry about what society thinks, but certain clothes should be avoided because, quite simply, they do not look good. As she advises her readers, and it's not that I think anyone should care what conclusions guys come to when they see a girl with so much side-boob, it really should be called front-boob, or what it says to that sweet old lady at the shops when someone's cut offs are so short she can see their c-section scar. It's just that it doesn't look all that good (Cullen, quoted at 30isthenewblack.com).

Clearly, Cullen does in fact care and hopes that you will too. Notwithstanding the fact that Cullen divorces the cultural and the aesthetic in this deeply ironic statement, I would note that her dictate to readers is as much about socially unacceptable "slutty" clothes as it is about the bodies that should or should not be allowed to wear them. Cullen is policing the boundaries of acceptable taste by painting a picture of disdainful displays that would injure "the sweet old lady" in the shops as visibly as "the c-section scar" on the lower abdomen of the woman on display. Marked and bulging in all the wrong places and, worse still, unabashedly putting their bodies on display, these women and girls must be put in their place – which is, according to these authors, out of sight. It should come as no surprise that the blogger who draws on this quote does so in the hopes of convincing her readers that there is a "fine hemline [and clearly body type] between stylish and 'skanky'" (www.30isthenewblack.com 2011).

The tenor of these narratives, as evidenced in the adjectives, descriptions, and outcomes discussed, illustrates strong feelings of disgust, anxiety, and repulsion. The nature of the problem is twofold. First, the bodies on display are viewed as un-presentable and indeed grotesque due to age – both in being too young and too old – as well as by being too round, scarred, or marked, and thus are unworthy of public exhibit. The second issue is related, but more pressing, because it speaks more directly to fears of contamination. As I have discussed at length in earlier chapters, sexualization is thought to be dangerous because of its infectious nature. This is why the problem of sexualization cannot be encapsulated by the issue of representation (e.g., there has been an increase in hypersexual advertisements and other popular media). Visual images, commodity objects, and poor role modeling produce sexualized desires and in so doing instantiate sexualized subjectivity – it is the public performance of this tainted identity and its desires which falls outside the parameters of middle-class taste, comportment, and thus respectable femininity. The fear at work in the sexualization literature is that the "fine line between stylish" (which signifies the middle class) and "skanky" (the embodiment of lower class) is no longer as clear as it should be. These two suppositions provide ingress into the classed nature of this discourse and its reliance on longstanding middle-class moral and medical preoccupations with the working class and "low culture" as well as social reform endeavors, which sought to inoculate the middle-class child from being corrupted by such stimuli. Cultural conceptions of low culture, which are currently referred to as "sexualized," "skanky," "prostitot," "raunchy," and "like a prostitute," and/or "brothel," feel natural because they carry with them deeply ingrained historical preoccupations and projections that conjoin the affective and the prescriptive. Such designations have a longstanding place within the Anglophone cultural imaginary as well as a deeply problematic legacy.

History, Affect, and Designations of High and Low

Peter Stallybrass and Allon White analyze the cultural construction of the "grotesque body" and low culture in England from the Renaissance to the Victorian period (Stallybrass and White 1986). The conflation of low culture with the working class, the colonized, and the insane formed the constitutive category against which the bourgeois body and its practices were constructed and reaffirmed. The production of low culture as disgusting, crass, and wanton was and is always already a site of ambivalence, a register through which both desire and revulsion get enacted. As Stallybrass and White note, "repugnance and fascination are the twin poles of the process in which a *political* imperative to reject and eliminate the debasing low conflicts powerfully and unpredictably with a desire for this Other" (Stallybrass and White 1986: 5).

This ambivalence is central to the construction of the colonialized as well as the domestic servant, the working-class male and the prostitute – all preoccupations of the bourgeois over the course of the nineteenth century. This paradoxical formation is situated in a "nexus of power and desire which regularly reappears in the ideological construction of the low-Other" (Stallybrass and White 1986: 5). Whereas the construction of the bourgeois body is modeled off the classical statue which has no orifices and is both rational and symmetrical, the body of the grotesque is all excess and fecundity with its "gaping mouth," "protuberant belly," "buttocks," "feet," and "genitals" (Stallybrass and White 1986: 22). As a result, the bodies of the poor, the colonized, the prostitute, and the insane were conceptualized as "mobile, split, [and] multiple" subjects of "pleasure in process of exchange" and thus "never closed off from either [the] social or ecosystemic context" (Stallybrass and White 1986: 22). For this reason they are both reviled and alluring. Revisiting the descriptions of sexualization and its various designations, one sees a striking similarity.

Historically, "the top attempts to reject and eliminate the bottom for reasons of prestige and status;" however, it soon discovers that "it depends upon that low Other . . . [and further] the top *includes* that low symbolically, as a primary eroticized constituent of its own fantasy life" (Stallybrass and White 1986: 22). The work of Edward Said and Ann Stoller further elucidates how this constitutive relationship has been central to the construction of the oriental other and the British colonist (Said 1979; Stoller 2002). At base, that which we deem disgusting, crass, or reckless is symbolically central to the production of the normal, clean, and morally righteous as well as the erotically seductive. Within the binary distinction between the classical and the grotesque, the excessive body is invoked both "defensively and offensively" because it is "fundamentally constitutive of the categorical sets" we use to make sense of both (Stallybrass and White 1986: 23). The foundational quality of the low and its contradictions were particularly evident in Anglophone anti-prostitution movements as well as social reformation movements dedicated to inoculating the bourgeois child against the contamination of urban street life over the course of

Figure 3.3 Posters from the American Social Hygiene Commission illustrate how the prostitute's body was collapsed with contagion and death. While sexually transmitted disease was a clear issue, it is noteworthy that death and disease was embodied female. It was her body that was both alluring and deadly. The classed coding of these images is found in the prostitute herself. Only the destitute, dangerous, and thus poor were constructed in this regard.

Source: University of Minnesota Library Social Welfare Archive

the nineteenth century (Stallybrass and White 1986; Mort 2000; Egan and Hawkes 2010). The prostitute, the impure or sexually knowing child, and the bawdy male were all sites of anxiety and acted as categories "in a metonymic chain of contagion which led back to the culture of the working classes" (Stallybrass and White 1986: 138; Egan and Hawkes 2010). However, the goal of eradication went hand in hand with the desire for transgression as evidenced in the practice of "slumming," consumption of prostitution, and the ubiquity of masturbation.

The middle- and upper-class body as pure, constrained, and rational was constructed by the "determining absent presence" of the working-class other; and as such, fantasies of the working-class body are foundational, albeit unacknowledged, to middle-class conceptions of the body, taste, and respectability (Macherey, quoted in Stallybrass and White 1986: 105). Within this construction, the working-class body is simultaneously polluting and dangerous as well as alluring. Jeffrey Weeks, Ann Stoller and others rightfully point out that attempts to erect boundaries between the bodies and practices of the middle class and those deemed "other" have rarely succeeded (e.g., neither in terms of sexual exploitation by middle-class men in cases of rape or harassment of women of color, poor women, colonized and slave women, nor in cases of consensual sex with secret affairs, or fantasies for girls from the other side of the tracks, etc.); and moreover, those who have had to bear the brunt of reform efforts have, more often than not, been the poor, people of color, and/or the working class (Hunt 1999; Mort 2000; Hall 2001; Weeks 2009; Egan and Hawkes 2010).

Although the thresholds of shame, embarrassment, and disgust which sustain and reproduce class divisions surrounding the body and designations of taste and respectability remain firmly in place when reading the literature on sexualization, the level of vitriol and extremity expressed about outcomes may point to the unsustainability of such divisions in our postmodern moment. The rhetorical tone in much of the popular writing renders visible the defensive quality of the discourse. Although the desire for separation has always been a losing battle, in part due to the excitement and allure of boundary crossing as well as the very nature of modern urban living (e.g., classes intermix in the cities), postmodern culture may render even the fantasy of separation far more implausible due to technology (e.g., social networking) and the various ways tweens and teens interact online. As a result, the fantasies which sustain the production of difference for the middle-class imaginary and its concomitant fantasies of childhood innocence, sexual respectability, and proper parenting may be under pressure due to increasing access children have to information and interactions via technology. YouTube, Twitter, Facebook, and other social media might be fueling a sense of anxiety due to the ease with which a child can secure access to information (violent, sexual, or otherwise) and, worse still, engage in interactions with the wrong kind of peer or adult. Middle-class anxiety may become more vigilant when

inoculation is thought to be impossible and may explain why outcomes are viewed in such extreme terms (e.g., oral sex for pay) and
why the future is cast in such dire terms.

Life on the Pole?

Linda Papadopoulos, author of the first British governmental report
on sexualization, states "The commodification of women and girls
is now so ingrained in our culture that glamour modelling and
lap-dancing are widely viewed not only as acceptable but in some
cases aspirational" (Papadopoulos 2010). Clive Hamilton offered a
similar argument on Australian television when he claimed that the
problem with sexualization is that girls aspire to be like "the slutty
celebrity images" they see in popular culture (Hamilton 2007).
Sexualization endangers because girls first consume and then seek
out these practices and, as a result, become the other. A crude
social constructionism and excessively simplistic vision of reception get perpetuated within this logic because consumption and
outcome are overdetermined. Through consumption, girls enact
or perform a type of femininity and eroticism that is outside the
boundaries of taste and comportment of the middle class. Through
this repeated stylization of the body, we are told that girls internalize and act *as if* they were the celebrities they watch or listen to.
In other words, mimicry and play are considered particularly dangerous because consumption will lead to transformation. In effect,
they become the grotesque. The young celebrities who are cited
as the bête noirs of this trend are Lindsay Lohan, Britney Spears,
Paris Hilton, Miley Cyrus, and, more recently, Snooki from
MTV's *Jersey Shore*. Although Paris Hilton has clearly come from
wealth, it is notable that Lohan, Spears, and Snooki are often seen
as coming from white working-class culture, and all are viewed as
emblematically outside the confines of respectability and upper-
class comportment.

Girls within this conception seem akin to automatons following the program set by sexualizing culture – they are only ever

responsive and passive in the extreme and become unequivocally that which they consume. Feminist sociologist Jessica Ringrose points out that "the extension of sex work as an economic possibility for middle-class girls (63% considering lap dancing) appears to be what is underpinning a great deal of the moral outrage, rather than a feminist concern to abolish sex work and prostitution full stop" (Ringrose 2013). The panic expressed by authors is not about sexualization per se; rather, it is "fuelled by a desire to return to a mythical space of sexual innocence for some children and girls" – those of the middle class (Ringrose 2013).[6] Polluted and polluting, it seems girls within these popular narratives are a danger to themselves and others. Given the manner in which sexualization is conceived and the actions it is said to induce, one sees rather quickly that the sexualized girl serves an important rhetorical purpose. Threatening middle-class sensibility, innocence, and even childhood itself, she becomes a clear and unambiguous enemy in the fight to save "our girls."

Although it often seems that tweenaged girls, once sexualized, happily jump the barricade of middle-class respectability and make a mad dash to the nearest strip club or video camera to lift their blouse for a *Girls Gone Wild* video, the empirical picture appears far more complicated (Kaiser Foundation 2003; Buckingham and Bragg 2004; Renold 2005; Herbenick et al. 2010; CDC 2011; Renold and Ringrose 2011; Ringrose and Renold 2012; Robinson 2012). As cited in chapter 1, the Centers for Disease Control and Prevention has recently presented data which shows that girls, of all races, are waiting longer to have intercourse and are, for the most part, very responsible when they decide to have sex (Bakalar 2012; Guttmacher Institute 2011). As the CDC notes, the percentage of boys and girls who have had penal vaginal intercourse is significantly lower today (43% of unmarried adolescent girls and 43% of unmarried boys) than their counterparts in 2002 (51% of girls and 60.4% of boys) (Bakalar 2012). When discussing their first sexual experience, 72% of teen girls stated it was with a steady partner (Bakalar 2012). The most common sexual practice is not oral (which is about 10% and 12% respectively for girls and boys aged 14–15) or anal sex (which comprised 4% of the sexual activities of 14–15-year-olds) – rather, it is what it is for every age category – masturbation (Herbenick et al. 2010; see also Fortenberry et al. 2010).

If the data, from many reliable sources, render claims made in the literature suspect, one must wonder what is behind the assertions that young girls are brokering oral sex for pay in suburbs, engaging in sexual behaviors on school buses and willfully taking part in a culture where "emotion-free sex is both expected and celebrated" (Oppliger 2008; Farley 2009a, 2009b; C. Hamilton 2009; M. Hamilton 2009a, 2009b; Klein 2009; Walter 2010). To this end, it seems particularly crucial to question the mythic quality and symbolic significance of sexualized girlhood, as a seemingly ubiquitous and voraciously promiscuous condition. This is not to say that media is innocuous or to deny that some girls feel increasingly pressured to fit within hegemonic parameters of beauty or sexuality. Rather, it is to ponder the usefulness of sexualization as it is currently conceptualized – as a constitutive category, one so burdened by middle-class fantasy, projection as well as fear, loathing, and disgust, that it requires extreme marginalization in order to sustain dominant conceptions of middle-class childhood and difference. Finally, the schism between the conceptualization of the problem and the data within the discourse on sexualization, as well as its use of hyperbole and affect, raises the specter of whether the problem of sexualization is simply a girl's problem, or whether the discourse is functioning as a metaphorical displacement for something else.

Class Displacement

Freud argued that displacement involves the unconscious transfer of feelings, from a particularly intense and intolerable idea to one that is less charged and thus easier for the individual to manage psychically (1900: 306). Most often, displacement runs along two "associative paths:" contiguity, which happens when a word is used that sounds like the idea which has been displaced in a dream;

and substitution via metaphor, which occurs when something comes to stand in for or replace that which has been disavowed. Within the sexualization literature, the sexualized girl is a substitution via metaphor – she represents middle-class impotence and the erosion of security in an increasingly insidious and predatory capitalist culture. What has been lost is the stability, or the fantasy of stability, of middle-class status (a class contagion of a different kind) rather than what she is on the surface – a representation of contagion due to transgressions in taste, comportment, and behavior. The sexualized girl is weighed down by middle-class fantasies about the eroticism of the working class as well as the middle-class rage, disgust, and impotence that gets displaced onto her and sexualization more generally. She is a clear enemy, one we can seemingly fight and overcome. Because the figure of the sexualized girl is made meaningful through longstanding cultural fantasies regarding the poor and low culture, seeing through these projections and displacements becomes all the more difficult. Nevertheless, deconstructing how the endangered girl subject is constructed within the literature grants ingress into how displacement may be at work in this discourse.

As I have illustrated already, the endangered girl in the discourse on sexualization is a white, middle-class, female, and heterosexual subject, whose subjectivity and behavior are defined through and against the sexualized. Within sexualization narratives, the girl endangered is an attempt to make the threat of contemporary culture more manageable because, in principle, she can be saved and thus represents a crisis averted. As a figure she helps to defend against impotence and alienation. This becomes more transparent when examining the logic of identification at work in the literature. Analyzing who or what gets defined as the problem ("raunchy," "skanky," "sexualized," and low-class objects and celebrities) as well as what happens as a result of identification (a desire for the sex industry, lack of ability to love now or in the future, promiscuity, emotional damage, etc.), we can see the classist nature of this discourse and its social-psychoanalytic implications. Valerie Walkerdine reminds us that social class "plays a central role in the regulation of femininity and the production of

Otherness" in discourses on the child (Walkerdine 1998: 171; see also Faulkner 2010). Innocence requires the bypassing of sexuality and it is for this reason that low culture "in so far as it presents the intrusion of adult sexuality into the sanitized space of childhood" is considered harmful to girls (Walkerdine 1998: 170).

The entire edifice of class, gender, race, and heterosexuality assumed in the discourse on sexualization becomes fragile at best, if the girl child is a sexual subject from the start or, better yet, if all girls are conceptualized as complex sexual citizens. Considering the manifold ways that reception is experienced and made meaningful across and within categories of race, class, gender, sexual identity, and religion would also render the current conceptualization of sexualization untenable. This raises the question, why do all of these differences get erased in the equation? Either the production of the endangered subject within the discourse is singular or the effects of sexualization are so monolithic that difference is eradicated. After plumbing the literature, I would contend that it is the former and not the latter.[7] The erasure of difference and the lack of attention to data can be read in two ways – both of which revolve around issues of social class. First, this discourse reflects a set of classist projections regarding taste, comportment, and eroticism, which uses the poor and the working class as the constitutive category against which middle-class girlhood and innocence get made intelligible. Second, the anxieties expressed over sexualization may also be a displacement for a far more disturbing and increasingly fragile socio-economic condition for the middle class. Both are beleaguered by adult projection and inspire a strong affective response. Adult projection carries with it the regulatory impetus of normalization and pathologization; as such, classifications of sexualization and innocence are never neutral and have political consequences. Notwithstanding, I believe it is worthwhile to understand the structural condition that might be providing the unconscious fuel to the fire of this endeavor – the socio-economic insecurities facing the middle class in our postmodern moment. Displacing fears and anxieties onto the sexualized girl may help ward off, at least temporarily, the destabilizing features of our contemporary cultural context and the material erosion of middle-class security in the Anglophone West. However, this defense requires the sexualized girl as a scapegoat.

Conclusion

Cultural critic and psychoanalyst Slavoj Zizek argues for a social-psychoanalytic conception of projection and displacement. He wants to expand the conceptualization of projection and displacement to include both the externalization of internal conflict onto an unsuspecting other as well as an externalization of or response to a particular external cultural condition (Zizek 2009). Accordingly, projection "bears witness to (and tries to cope with) the fact that I am originally decentered, part of an opaque network whose meaning and logic elude my control" (Zizek 2009: 9). Within this context, projection functions as an attempt to "provide the answer to 'What does society want from me?', to unearth the meaning of the murky events in which I am forced to participate" (Zizek 2009: 9). *I argue that displacement represents the inability to incorporate the gravity of such an answer.* Thus, projection and displacement provide temporary solace against that which we cannot bear as well as a more psychically palatable way to negotiate a condition over which we have little or no control.[8] As I have shown thus far, these defenses often spur untenable and deeply problematic projections about the other. They help foster rigid binaries in order to create an illusion of purity, difference, and distinction (e.g., good and evil, normal and abnormal, sinner and saint, monster and sanctified).

When reading the literature, we are told that sexualization creates a new mode of subjectivity wherein formerly innocent girls become "trashy" and take pleasure in bawdy displays and sexually salacious behavior; this impingement upon middle-class respectability, taste, and finally subjectivity represents, for most authors, a monstrous outcome. Nevertheless, it is my contention that the sexualized girl may be a metaphor for something else. She portends a future wherein the boundaries of middle-class status, security, and livelihood are transgressed and transformed by an increasingly insidious form of capital. In this sense, it is not the erosion of middle-class taste and comportment which is the problem, but shifts in the formation of capital which erode middle-class aspirations and achievement. This discourse is driven, in part, by the possible dissension of the middle class into the ranks of the working class, or worse, working poor due to an increasingly fragile economic future. The sexualized girl may be read as the embodiment of a porous, defiled, and corroded social status – rather than simply as a corrupted mode of middle-class girlhood. Either way, she personifies a deeply disturbing future and one that must be stopped.

The sexual child has often served as both a displacement for cultural anxiety as well as a site of seemingly manageable intervention in an increasingly anxiety-producing cultural condition (Romesberg 2008; Egan and Hawkes 2010). Consequently, one should wonder whether our increasingly unforgiving form of capital and its impact on the middle class has played a part, although by no means the only part, in the production of an exaggerated displacement through the figure of the sexualized child. As I have endeavored to illustrate throughout this chapter, this dynamic becomes more transparent when analyzing how sexualization is conceptualized within popular narratives and the extent to which this discourse is being propelled by adult projections which draw on historical conceptions of class, taste, comportment, and gender, and which are fueled by affect. If we take these data seriously, we understand rather quickly that girls are not nearly as wild, promiscuous, or out of control as supposed in the literature on sexualization. Lurking underneath the fears of class contagion in the sexualization literature is a very real sociological condition with rising wealth gaps, a rapidly dissolving social safety net, changes in global capitalism, and increasing disparity between rich and poor that have, over the last decade, come together to dismantle the economic security of the middle class. In the face of all of this, does sexualization and the form of girlhood it supposedly engenders offer a far more unequivocal figure to fight against, thereby giving sexualization advocates some semblance of control in an increasingly uncontrollable context? I believe that the answer to this question is yes.

While, on one level, this response makes sense given the current socio-economic climate in the United States and the United Kingdom and the instability it produces, nevertheless it should not mitigate the pernicious assumptions regarding class, gender, sexuality, and race which underpin it. Although it might provide temporary solace by crafting a common enemy, it also produces a defiled and defiling other to secure its credibility. As cultural critics, we need to be extremely cautious about creating a discourse of sexual protection spurred primarily by affect and hyperbole; while it may be effective in generating solidarity, it might also unwittingly create a movement which marginalizes some girls in order to protect others. Projection and the affective response it engenders hinder a critical interrogation of the evocative nature of the extreme claims at work in the discourse on sexualization and the classism, racism, and ultimately sexism that it can inspire. Equally important, it also displaces our anxiety from a structural condition that is far more elusive and unwieldy, but may actually represent the problem. If this is the case, then the discourse on sexualization may unwittingly fall into the trap of populism, albeit in a more disguised and socially palatable (due to its derision of the poor and low culture) form.

In the final chapter, I turn my attention to how adult ambivalence regarding the eroticism of children, tweens, and teens may also limit the conceptualization of sexualization and unwittingly inspire a form of discomfort and loathing which gets projected on the girls who are deemed sexualized within the literature.

4

Unmanageable Bodies, Adult Disgust, and the Demand for Innocence

Mastery through sublimation, diverting the sexual energy away from its sexual goal to higher cultural aims, succeeds with a minority, and with them only intermittently; while the period of passionate youth is precisely that in which it is most difficult to achieve . . . Experience shows that the majority of those who compose our society are constitutionally unfit for the task of abstinence.

Sigmund Freud (1908a), Civilized sexual morality and modern nervous illness

Today young women have embraced their own degrading objectification. Seeming to have abandoned the hope of real equality with men, women and girls enact prostitution. Pole dancing, once the exclusive province of women in strip clubs, has moved to women's homes and exercise classes. Lap dancing and pole dancing have become mainstreamed as women's and girls' sexuality.

Melinda Tankard Reist (2009b), *Getting Real: Challenging the Sexualization of Girls*

Introduction

Comparing the quotes above, it seems that we have found ourselves in an inverted cultural landscape. The impact and severity of the sexual codes described by Sigmund Freud only a hundred years ago seem almost anthropological – the misplaced prudery of a bygone era or, for some, a distant memory of a much simpler and more wholesome time. Casting our perspective backward, it is impossible not to see that the sexual landscape critiqued by Freud has been radically altered. In the Anglophone West, the proliferation of media and technology, movements demanding the rights and recognition of marginalized populations since the 1960s, shifts in child-rearing practices and family configuration, the legalization of birth control and abortion, increasing mobility and global tourism, the emergence of HIV and AIDS globally, the acceleration of global capital, and the rise and influence of neoconservatives and evangelical Christianity on policy making have all molded and informed our understanding and experience of sex in society (Hawkes 2004; Siedman 2009; Weeks 2009). In the midst of our ultra modern moment and the mainstreaming of sex it entails, it is hard to imagine the rules and sexual decorum imposed in Freud's modernity (Attwood 2006, 2009). While middle-class Victorian girls may have been confined by high collars, corsets, and cultural demands for sexuality deferred, the tweenaged girls of today, as we are warned by Melinda Tankard Reist and others writing on sexualization, have found themselves in far more dire straits. Media messages mainstreaming "lap dancing" and "prostitution" have hijacked innocence and replaced it with promiscuous action (Farley 2009a, 2009b; Reist 2009a: 11). On the face of it, it would seem that we are talking about apples and oranges. However, if one scratches beneath the surface, continuities and connections become far more apparent.

Upon first reading, one might also say that the concerns raised by authors writing on sexualization resonate with Freud – contemporary civilization and its effects on sexuality foster psychopathological symptoms, albeit emerging from a different source, the media, and capitalism and produce a different set of outcomes – the precocious activation of compulsive sexuality in tweenaged girls. However, this interpretation would ignore a key theoretical pillar of psychoanalysis – that children are, by their very nature, erotic beings. As Freud argues in his essay on "The sexual enlightenment of children," written in 1907, "the new-born infant brings sexuality with it into the world; certain sexual sensations attend its development while at the breast and during early childhood, and only very few children would seem to escape some kind of sexual activity and sexual experience before puberty" (Freud 1907/1963: 19). As such, infantile sexuality "comes about spontaneously from internal causes" (Freud 1905a: 57).[1] While society or other external forces may impinge upon a child's activities and feel discomfort or anxiety when it is on display, libido is already active in the child and thus its mere presence should not be considered a manifestation of pathology.[2] Freud's discussion of infant eroticism and the importance of sexuality more generally is certainly controversial, and it would be tempting to spend the entire chapter arguing for its merits, as tempered by feminist psychoanalysts such as Jessica Benjamin, Susie Orbach, and Juliet Mitchell (which I have done in earlier publications), but the focus of this analysis lies elsewhere – adult fixations and panics about the child and its sexuality (Benjamin 1998; Mitchell 2000; Orbach 2005; Egan 2006; Egan and Hawkes 2010). Nevertheless, it is important to note that the psychoanalytic conception of the child as a sexual being is axiomatic in this analysis. My substantive interest for this chapter returns us again to the question of the applicability of Freud, and psychoanalysis more generally, to the question of sexualization.

Although it is certainly the case that the sexual landscape of the Anglophone West has changed (in terms of representation and an expansion of culturally acceptable practices and identities), many of the epistemological assumptions guiding dominant cultural discourses produced by adults on the nature, potential corruption, and outcome of the child and its sexuality have remained extraordinarily consistent (Darby 2005; Egan and Hawkes 2008, 2009, 2010; Faulkner 2010; Hawkes and Egan 2012). A desire to unpack the emotion work of this discourse and the various ways in which the figure of the sexual child is rendered intelligible by adults within it (as a compulsive, hypersexual, and pathologized girl subject) resonates with the conceptual focus of a social-psychoanalytic approach. Its emphasis on mechanisms of shame, disgust, projection, anxiety, ambivalence, repression, defense mechanisms, and unconscious conflicts offers a particularly compelling explanatory framework for interrogating our culture's panic and preoccupation with childhood sexuality as it is currently deployed in the discourse on sexualization. Psychoanalysis provides the tools with which to make sense of the taken-for-granted assumptions of this discourse and, equally important, it can offer cultural critics an understanding of its place within our larger cultural imaginary. Psychoanalytic insights shed light on the longstanding Anglophone desire for the figure of the sexually innocent child; and, even more provocatively, it grants ingress into our equally arresting attachment or cathexis for the Janus face of innocence – the sexually compulsive, erotically dangerous, and sexually defiled child.

As I have shown throughout this text, recent writing on sexualization argues that female tweens are sexualized as a result of media, advertising, and commodities.[3] Besieged by cultural dangers heretofore unseen (the rapid proliferation of Internet pornography, increasingly sexual magazines, celebrities such as Britney Spears, Lindsay Lohan, or Miley Cyrus, advertising campaigns selling salacious and inappropriate clothing), girls are surrounded by a toxic environment of sexualization that is almost impossible to escape. As conservative Mona Charen laments, "when girls barely out of diapers are encouraged to wear make-up, skin-tight miniskirts, and push-up bras, we've left the realm of wanting to look pretty and gone into something sick and tawdry . . . fathers and mothers, protect your girls' innocence" (Charen 2007). Sexualizing materials encourage and, as a consequence, are said to produce sexualized action (APA 2007; Rush and La Nauze 2006a; Durham 2008; Oppliger 2008; Klein 2009; Fyfe 2008; Papadopoulos 2010). Sexualized behaviors emerge in the following manner: mimicry, internalization, and finally self-destructive impulses that impinge upon the present and shape the future. Anti-sexualization advocates deploy a causal "hypodermic model," which states that media representations produce universal effects in tween girls (Egan and Hawkes 2008, 2010). The end point of our morally bankrupt and patriarchal culture is a genera-tion of girls who have "abandoned the hope of real equality" and instead embrace "their own degrading objectification" and worse still enact sexual acts ranging from lap dancing on school buses, having casual sex with multiple partners, performing oral sex for pay at parties, engaging in intergenerational sex, and enacting prostitution (APA 2007; Rush and La Nauze 2006b; Durham 2008; Oppliger 2008; Farley 2009a, 2009b; Reist 2009a: 20). The extremity of the scope and damage put forward by activists attempts to strike fear and anxiety in the reader and draws on disgust and shame in the service of its message. Adult inaction, we are told, is tantamount to child abuse.

Deconstructing this discourse and its departure from the empiri-cal picture offered by much of the qualitative and quantitative work on girls, popular culture, and sexual behavior raises impor-tant questions about what else might be lying beneath its stated goals. Thus far, I have made the case that the peril of sexualiza-tion is a metaphor for larger social instabilities regarding gender, sexuality, class, and race – that the girl is, in effect, a displacement for a more unmanageable social situation. Deploying longstand-ing Anglophone preoccupations regarding race, class, gender, and sexuality adds affective fuel to the fire and makes challenging the production of pathological girlhood all the more difficult. If the postmodern condition in the Anglophone West is destabilizing due to its speed, fragmentation, and increasingly insidious forms of capitalism, then displacement, as a defense against this onslaught, is understandable. As I have shown, the discourse on sexualization represents such a defense by offering us a clear and unambiguous enemy to fight as well as some hope for a different future. The girl endangered is more chimera than material; she represents the crises of a particular group (white and middle-class) and its longing for stability in an insecure context. It is for this reason that the lens of concern is focused on a fairly narrow subset of girls (white, middle-class, and heterosexual) to the exclusion and marginalization of others. Up to this point, I have examined how this discourse draws on various registers of ambivalence surrounding race, class, gender, and sexuality. This final chapter examines adult ambivalence surrounding the child and its sexuality in the hope of illuminating the allure of the sexually endangered and sexually corrupted child within sexualization narratives.

Unpacking the unspoken (unconscious) dynamics at work in this conception of the sexual child within the Anglophone cultural discourses highlights the evocative nature of such assumptions and how they work to render other considerations (such as the child as a sexual citizen) untenable. Revisiting the idea of the armature, earlier chapters attempted to render visible the taken-for-granted ideological and epistemological assumptions at work in the construction of the sexualized girl. This chapter explores another epistemological and affective line in this conceptual structure by examining dominant cultural conceptions of infantile eroticism and how they underpin narratives on sexualization and the construction of the sexualized girl.[4] Exploring how the sexualized girl is made meaningful, as an evocative object, will help illuminate why we are so attached to her and why she feels so truthful even when juxtaposed against a far more complicated picture.

Psychoanalyst Christopher Bollas uses the term "evocation" to explain how objects can grab hold of someone in ways that do not always seem to make sense (i.e., a picture of an ex-lover who hurt you; a salt shaker from your grandmother's house; or a figure in a comic book or protagonist in a novel), but are powerful nonetheless (Bollas 2009). Such objects provoke thinking (e.g., of our family history, or about something like warfare) and inspire feelings (e.g., loneliness, love, or rage). Evocation is not about rationality, but the realm of feelings, the unconscious and corporeal response (Bollas 2009). It is compelling because it *feels* authentic, important, and truthful, not necessarily because it *is* authentic or truthful. To this end, unraveling the evocative quality of an object exposes why it speaks to us and why we find it so intriguing. It also sheds light on the emotional and visceral response it produces. However, because the origins of our attachments are, at times, unconscious, they can be elusive. Evocation is rarely simple or unequivocal; rather, it is a dynamic response that is often conflicted, paradoxical, and ambivalent, but deeply felt and requires critical reflection and inference to pull apart its various threads.

Adult projection and transference are clearly at work within the discourse on sexualization, and provide a defense against the insecurity and discomfort that arises in particular moments of cultural turmoil and transition. However, a cultural analysis alone cannot adequately answer why our culture is so deeply besotted with the sexualized child and the defilement of sexual innocence. For example, why haven't we moved on to another equally compelling figure or series of figures? As I discussed briefly in chapter 2, James Kincaid's research in *Erotic Innocence: The Culture of Child Molesting* exposes an unspoken, but historically trenchant, contradiction in the Anglophone conception of childhood – we are deeply attached to the stories we tell about the sexual exploitation or sexual defilement of children (Kincaid 1998). We would not continuously revisit these tales "of the exploitation of the child's body if we didn't wish to have it told . . . [this story] keeps the subject hot so we can disown it while welcoming it in the back door" (Kincaid 1998). In other words, it is no coincidence that the Anglophone construction of the child as both innocent and sentimental (and thus categorically different from the adult) enthralls – this difference is both alluring and disavowed. Within this context, protection from defilement becomes an acceptable narrative through which we can endlessly look upon and think about the child and sex.

Our penchant for eroticizing "empty innocence seems to have left us ashamed and transfixed, unable to change and unable to resist the cultural directives that instruct us to long for children precisely in reference to what they do not have" (Kincaid 1998: 17). The denial at work in this cultural preoccupation keeps our attention centered squarely on the need to protect the child, as a figure, from sex, while ignoring actual children and the conditions of childhood which fall outside of our cultural fantasies of "kids with sticky kisses and fistfuls of dandelions" such as poverty or neglect (Kincaid 1998: 109). Our "obsessive focus on protection" has a paradoxical effect – it "saturate[s] children with a sexual discourse that inevitably links children, sexuality and erotic appeal," but does so in a way that obfuscates adults as the ideological authors of this construction (Kincaid 1998: 101). Kincaid wonders, is this "a destructive psychic drama we have inherited and cannot find a way to escape?" (Kincaid 1998: 109).

Taking Kincaid's insights seriously requires that we think about adult fascination as one of the forces driving the discourse on sexualization. It would be patently false to say that the sexual exploitation of children does not exist. Kincaid argues the opposite – that our representations of childhood are deeply problematic, almost pedophilic. His assessment of our cultural penchant for eroticizing innocence raises important questions about the discourse on sexualization and its use of affect. Nevertheless, I argue that a slight revision is needed to address the schism between the hyperbolic outcomes forwarded in the discourse on sexualization and the empirical literature. Our "obsessive focus on protection" may also have its origins in moments when we come into contact with a child who is autoerotic, unashamed, omnipotent, and curious. If the child is constructed as that which is asexual, but always already on the verge of sexual corruption from something or someone suspect, then any manifestation of something different is destabilizing and calls into question the boundaries between the adult and child and may ignite a host of ambivalent feelings such as disgust, anger, anxiety, or longing which must be disavowed. If our interactions with children can evoke a deeply ambivalent reaction which must be disavowed, then our "obsessive focus on protection" may also be a defensive posture against the resuscitation of that ambivalence. If this is the case, then the production of innocence is a response to childhood eroticism rather than a categorical quality of childhood that gets sullied or destroyed by contact with a corrupt catalyst. Deflecting the adult need for difference by transforming it into discussions of corruption and endangerment is an attempt to maintain boundaries and keep ambivalent feelings at bay. The longevity and staying power of the sexually endangered or defiled child is a symptom of unresolved conflict in adults rather than the danger of perverse enactments by children. Within sexualization narratives, this unresolved conflict is made manifest in the affective undercurrent of loathing and guilt at work in the construction of the sexualized girl and her innocent counterpart.

Appearing on the US morning television program, *The Early Show*, Therapist Jane Greer summarizes sexualization and its corrupting qualities when she states,

> Well, [girls] all want to grow up. I mean, remember when we were young? We wanted to wear our mother's clothes, step into her shoes. And now being grown-up, a la Lindsay Lohan means being sexy, low cut jeans, middriffs. And that's what they want." (Greer on *The Early Show*, quoted in Raezler 2008).

Seeking a life on the lap-dance couch or the pole, girls mimic "crotch flashing," "topless posing," "slutty" celebrities, and apparently offer "oral" and "lesbian" sex in their unyielding quest for male attention. Sexualization erodes the barrier between child and adult as Susan Linn notes, "girls are [being] encouraged to act like teenagers just a few years after shedding their diapers" (Linn 2009: 49). Nevertheless, the hyperbole at work in the narratives and the extremity of action discussed also speaks to a lack of shame, self-control, the desire for exhibitionism, and extreme narcissism – all qualities that also speak to the lack of sociability of early childhood. It is my contention that the figure of the sexualized girl draws upon our cultural discomfort, disgust, and preoccupation with infantile eroticism. The sexualized girl is constructed through a range of middle–class fantasies as well as through our cultural disquiet regarding the polymorphously perverse child.

If adult frenzy surrounding the sexual child and its innocence is an attempt to ward off feelings of the shame, disgust, or possibly the pleasure associated with the polymorphous perversity of the pre-Oedipal period, then our cultural discourses regarding the child and its sexuality become a far more complex social phenomenon. However, given the hazy nature of our earliest period of life, it is important to note that adult memories and understanding of that time are through the lens of adult perception and/or fantasy.

Consequently, adult perceptions of the child and its sexuality may often suffer from what Michael Good calls a screen reconstruction (Good 1998). Screen reconstructions are perceptions that *feel truthful and are experienced as such*, but are more often than not defensive in nature and thus fantasmatic. They are a mechanism we use to grapple with the intolerable. Although Good explores this concept in a therapeutic context, I believe it has use as a social-psychoanalytic framework as well. If dominant cultural narratives (and such cultural narratives are reflections, at least in part, of our cultural imaginary) inform our sense of the past and present, then cultural ambivalence regarding specific issues may shape our perceptions, and promote particular visceral responses particularly in contexts that are confusing or disconcerting. As I have noted already, Anglophone cultural conceptions of the child are deeply ambivalent – the child is both a site of sentimentality and suspicion (Walkerdine 1998; Cross 2004). This extends into our conceptions of childhood sexuality as a site of both innocence and compulsivity. Both rely upon the construction of childhood as something distinct and different from the adult. It is my contention that our cultural imaginary fosters a particular form of screen reconstruction of the child and the tween that we draw on when we encounter behaviors that we find intolerable, disgusting, and alluring. What if the child's behavior grates against our desire for innocence and sweetness? Do we then project onto it our desires, preoccupations, and fixations? Do we need a vision of innocence to defend against our ambivalence? Must we split the child into innocent and knowing in order to maintain our conception of childhood? Unearthing the complex mechanisms that may be underlying these projections is the focus of the next section. By analyzing the use of the language, tone, and visual imagery deployed within published work on sexualization, I illustrate the ambivalence about the child, its sexuality, and the ideals of innocence at work within this call for protection. Prior to discussing this, it is important to understand the pre-Oedipal period in order to illuminate why it may evoke anxiety or discomfort in some adults who are witnessing it.

The Return of the Repressed and the Desire to Repeat

In contrast to "the popular view of the sexual instinct [which says] that [eroticism] is absent in childhood," Freud offers a radical departure,

> that the germs of sexual impulses are already present in the new-born child and that these continue to develop for a time, but are then over-taken by a progressive process of suppression [latency] . . . it seems however that the sexual life of children usually emerges in a form accessible to observation round about the third or fourth year of life (Freud 1905a: 42–3).

To this end, "the constitutional disposition of the child is by far more variegated than we might have expected . . . it deserves to be called 'polymorphously perverse'" (Freud 1905b). Departing from the epistemological assumptions underlying dominant discourses, the child's sexuality is "already present in the new born" and its eroticism is not conflated with the development of its sex organs. Whereas sexual organ development occurs during early fetal development, "the early efflorescence of infantile sexual life" takes place around age three (Freud 1905a: 43). The implication of this distinction is important – if eroticism is not tethered to physiological maturation, then it opens the possibility that it is not quiescent until puberty; and as a result, its manifestation is not necessarily abhorrent.

Sexual instincts, for Freud, are situated at the intersection of the mental and the physical – they are the psychical representation of a continuously flowing source of stimulus – as opposed to a response to a singular source of excitation (Freud 1905a). The pleasure principle, which involves the drive toward the eradication of tension or unpleasure, is central to his conception; infantile sexuality emerges from and in relation to pleasure sparked from "vital somatic functions" (Freud 1905a: 48). It is the pleasurable feeling the child receives from the satiation of its basic needs, such as hunger, that it later seeks to reproduce on its own. Moreover, a child's sexuality is instantiated through its interactions with the mother's body (Egan and Hawkes 2010). In her daily care of the infant, the mother produces a continuous source of excitation and pleasurable feelings in the various erotogenic zones of her child's body, which it seeks to reproduce later (Freud 1907/1963). A child's sexual aim and its search for a sexual object are formed in an analogous fashion; they are both created "in connection with the bodily functions necessary for self-preservation" (1923a: 50). Pleasure for the child then unfolds in a dual fashion: from the satiation of its basic needs and through somatic stimulation (Egan and Hawkes 2010). During the pre-Oedipal phase of its sexual life, a child's sexual impulse is "freely exercised" in both aim and desire; moreover, both its aims and objects are born out if its dependency upon and relationship with its mother and thus are beset by jealousy, pleasure, turmoil, and ultimately trauma when giving up the Oedipal object (Freud 1908b/2006: 17; 1924/1997).

Until shame and inhibition emerge later (under the educative influence and socialization), children experience no natural barrier to activities or impulses many adults consider repulsive in later life: the gulf between humans and animals, excreta, the distinction between the sexes, pleasure in the autoerotic nature of the entire body, and incestuous desires (Freud 1905b, 1908b, 1923b/1997). Deeply curious, children are guided by "an autonomous investigative drive" that is both sensual and sexual (1908b/2006: 226). Lacking the constraint imposed by the superego, children are at the mercy of the id and thus "amoral" and in need of guidance and control by their parents or other parental substitutes (Freud 1933: 77). Although Freud argues that the efflorescence of childhood comes to a close during latency, he also notes that this is not always the case. This statement spurred Wilhelm Reich's supposition that the period of latency is not a biological given but rather a cultural requirement; then the "polymorphous," "variegated," and "autoerotic" nature of the pre-Oedipal moment is never fully absented during the period of quiescence known as latency (Reich 1933/1972; Freud 1905a: 48).

Although Freud believed that anyone (even those who were vehement in their claims about "the seraphic innocence of the child's mind") who observed a child could not dispute their lack of shame and autoerotic nature – it is clear from the materials I have reviewed and the often controversial reception that Freud's work receives (then and now) that repression is quite common (Freud 1933: 34; Marcus 2000; Thwaites 2007). While one could argue that many adults might accept that the "germs of the sexual impulse" may be present at birth, the voracious quality of infantile eroticism in terms of its aims and objects and its relationship to maternal touch seems to be repugnant for many adults (Marcus 2000). As a result, this period of polymorphous perversity is often repressed and thus vehemently "denied" by "civilized" societies (Freud 1908b/2006). Stallybrass and White argue that part of this repression involved displacing such perversities onto the poor, the prostitute, the insane, and the colonized (Stallybrass and White 1986). As this book illustrates, this denial is as salient in our contemporary culture as it was for the Victorians. We can begin to understand how adults look back upon this period through an analysis of the qualities and motivations they project onto children, and thus we can have a better picture of the compulsions driving cultural attempts to censor this period of childhood.

Adults cannot easily grasp the ways in which children experience or make meaning of early childhood and as a result misperceive a child's motivations and/or actions (Ferenczi 1949/1951). Salvador Ferenczi argues that adults often have a different vision, language, and understanding, what he terms a "confusion of tongues," that colors their perceptions of the child and its actions (Ferenczi 1949/1951). This confusion causes conflicts and, in extreme cases, trauma for children subject to adult misperceptions and the actions they may inspire (Ferenczi 1949/1951). Ferenczi's provocative insights led me to wonder whether seeing the polymorphous activities of children could trigger a return of the repressed, producing anxiety, disgust, and possibly titillation in adults. Why? Because the return of the repressed is re-experienced through adult perception and for this reason is distorted. Adult perception is not simply idiosyncratic, nor is it entirely predetermined – it is shaped by character, culture, and history (personal and socio-historical). This is why not all adults or cultures (or even all adults within the same

culture) will react in the same way. Nevertheless, what my analysis renders visible is that, within the narratives on sexualization,
adults perceive that tweenaged eroticism produces a combustible,
compulsive, and almost monstrous outcome. This is evidenced
in the claims that sexualization produces the desire for intergenerational sex, objectification, and "the object of men's sexual
fantasies," and active participants in the sex industry as "smiling
strippers and escorts" (Farley 2009b: 144, 159). The return of the
repressed at work within this discourse is inferred by the adjectives
used, which reflect disgust, anxiety, and repulsion. Because this
discourse is one of protection, the loathing and repugnance found
within it must be defended against and projected outward toward
the offending cause – technology, media, and clothing. Although
authors state that the goal of the movement is the empowerment
and "re-personalisation of girls," an analysis of the behaviors and
descriptions deployed within this discourse belies this claim (Reist
2009a: 18).

It is important to note that repressed desires or fantasies never
really vanish or get "destroyed;" rather, they return in a disguised
fashion – in this case the sexualized girl (Freud 1905b). Moreover,
"repression is not an event that occurs once;" rather, it "requires a
permanent expenditure of energy" to keep its contents and long-
ings at bay (Freud 1925: 157). The desire to render impotent the
return of the repressed is a wish that goes unfulfilled because it is
reintroduced and repeated through adult interactions (in terms of
mother/child interactions and in observations of other children)
with children who enact autoeroticism and fantasies of omnipo-
tence. Adult engagement with childhood sexuality collides with
the revulsion that resides beneath a thin pellicle of repression and
this creates more anxiety and another attempt at repression – a
pattern of repetition compulsion.

Edward Bibring notes that repetition compulsion is a complex
dynamic where one seeks to recreate and thus repeat trauma while
simultaneously longing for its resolution and thus a return to a
pre-traumatic state or situation (Bibring 1943). Although this may,
at first, seem paradoxical, it reveals the ambivalent nature humans
have to trauma: it is painful, but familiar and thus seductive. The

vicissitudes of affect underpinning the tweenaged girl (of seeking to eradicate the impact of trauma vis-à-vis sexualizing culture while also being attached to the figure of the sexualized girl) are central to the literature on sexualization. Through their construction of defiled innocence via the sexually imperiled child, activists unconsciously recreate the figure and condition (sexualization and thus the sexualized child) they seek to eradicate and prevent within the narrative. This ambivalence is illustrated in the primary contradiction at the heart of sexualization literature – that it is impossible to stem the tide of sexualization (because it is akin to poisoned air), but that it is also preventable with the right tools offered by authors and activists. This paradox illuminates how the fight against sexualization is an attempt to repress polymorphous perversity through the fantasy of the innocent child – however, the manner in which sexuality is conceptualized (as catalyzed by a ubiquitous and corrupt external force) renders the fantasy of innocence implausible at best and impossible at worst. The logic upon which this discourse rests *de facto* ensures that the trauma (the sexual child) remains an open wound – one that is ready and waiting for another failed attempt at suture in the near future.

One may surmise that, although the discourse produced by activists outwardly advocates the end of sexualization, underneath it requires the presence of the sexualized girl. As such, the discourse against sexualization, like its historical counterparts, enacts a repetition compulsion. If this repetition compulsion were conscious, this discourse and the movement it supports could not be maintained. It is for this reason that the figure of the child within these narratives is unconsciously split, in the Kleinian sense, between the sexualized or knowing child and the innocent or asexual child.

Melanie Klein and other object relations thinkers such as Joan Riviere illustrate how infants and adults engage in "splitting" and projective identification to help defend against feelings of hatred, aggression, and panic that they are unable to acknowledge as their own (Klein 1937; Riviere 1937). According to Klein, the infant experiences love and satiation as well as the terror, anxiety, and rage associated with hunger and other unmet needs in its earliest infancy. These early, and inevitable, experiences create attempts to quell discomfort – however, this situation produces deep frustration and even rage. As a result, the child's relation to the mother, its "first love [for the mother via the partial object of the breast] is already disturbed at its roots by destructive impulses" (Klein 1937: 60). Unable to handle these overwhelming and terrifying feelings of frustration and rage, the baby splits its (internal and thus fantasy) part object, the breast, into one that is benevolent, loving, and all giving, and another that is evil and withholding.[5] In effect, the evil object becomes a dumping ground for feelings that are overstimulating and unacceptable. This helps babies manage their destructive impulses which become "tantamount to death wishes" by projecting their feelings onto an object other than the self (Klein 1937: 61). This type of splitting is what Melanie Klein terms a paranoid schizoid form. Although this is a mechanism that starts in infancy, it has a place in our arsenal of defense mechanisms throughout life.

Later in infancy the child comes to understand the internal object in a more holistic manner (not just as the breast, but as the mother), and as one that provokes both benevolent and frustrating experiences and is worthy of love. During fits of distress and rage, the infant may fantasize that she "has really destroyed" the object and feel tremendous guilt as the cost of her annihilation (Klein 1937: 61). As a result, the infant engages in another type of omnipotent fantasy wherein she attempts to put "the bits" of the destroyed object "together again" and thus repair what she has broken apart (Klein 1937: 61). This reparation will ensure the object's love and lovability in the future. Klein calls this fantasy a depressive one, and it is foundational to maturation. However, the question becomes what happens to our destructive impulses and the desire to destroy that which frustrates and denies us in adulthood?

As Joan Riviere notes, feelings of love and hate are the territory of our unconscious and only a small part "ever becomes known to our conscious minds" (Riviere 1937: 10). Moreover, the "hate, aggression, envy, jealousy and greed felt and expressed" by adults "are all derivatives, and usually extremely complicated derivatives, of this primary experience and of the necessity to master it"

(Riviere 1937: 10). It is for this reason that we go back to these early forms of splitting and use them as defense mechanisms in adulthood. I contend that the manner in which the sexual child is conceptualized in anti-sexualization literature is such a "complex derivative," though by no means the only one, of these primary experiences. Both paranoid schizoid and depressive defenses are at work in the discourse on sexualization.

The unconscious frustrations and shame associated with the aims and objects of our earliest years get projected onto the knowing, corrupt, or sexualized child. Into this figure is dumped the adult fantasies and projections regarding the pre-Oedipal period (Freud 1908b). This splitting is extraordinarily palpable in the adjectives used to describe the sexual girl within the anti-sexualization literature. Writers, feminist and non-feminist alike, have called her a "skank," a "prostitot," a "kinderwhore," and "sex bait," have said she wears clothes touched by the "skank fairy" and as a result she dresses "like a stripper" or wears "skank chic," "hooker-wear," "porn chic," or "trailer park fashion," and engages in "freaky dancing," "sexually precocious," or "slutty" behavior, and actively takes part in "casual fellatio at parties," "lap dancing," and even "prostitution" (Reist 2009a: 14; Farley 2009a: 119; Oppliger 2008: 2, 4, 9; Rush 2009: 7; Durham 2008: 82; Hamilton 2007: 59; Rivenbark 2006: 28–9). Since this happens "just a few years after shedding diapers," to children as young as three, sexualization impacts the objects with which she surrounds herself (Linn 2009: 49; Lafsky 2009). She enjoys playing with toys that resemble "prostitutes," "sluts," or "hookers" and watches shows like *The Real World, Jersey Shore,* and *Gossip Girl* (Kilbourne, in Cabrera 2007; see also Oppliger 2008: 23; Crowley 2006). She embraces her own "degradation" and longs for a life "on the stripper pole," seeks to "please at any cost" because she, at base, wants to "attract attention" (APA 2007; M. Hamilton 2009a: 57). The implications of this splitting become more remarkable when it is set against the definition of the term "prostitot" from the *Urban Dictionary,* a wiki created primarily by young men between the ages of 18 and 24 (a website which could easily be called misogynist):

Prostitot (n.)

1. A young girl with too much makeup and not enough clothes.
2. An obviously underage girl who dresses like a whore . . .
    The junior high just let out . . . look at all them prostitots . . .
3. A child resembling, or working as a prostitute. Usually the result of admiring britney, xtina or their skanky-ass mother.
    Stacy put on her assless chaps and went out to play on the swings/pick up men. Fuckin prostitot . . .
4. (n) 1. Young girl who dresses in a scandelous [sic] manner. 2. Female preteen intent on attracting adult men.
    That prostitot is showing her diaper.
5. A dyslexic 12-year-old girl who thinks she's 21 and dresses accordingly. Thongs, tank tops, short skirts and other revealing clothes are the hallmarks of the prostitot.
    Prostitot: Want a lapdance?
    Guy: What are you, like 12? I'm no pedophile
    Urban Dictionary (2008)

Looking up other words used in the anti-sexualization literature reveals a similar pattern. Both prefigure the sexualized girl as damaged, insatiable, and dangerous. The hypersexuality projected onto her makes her a figure of repulsion and fear. This fantasmatic projection is then re-introjected back into the ego as a site of danger and corruption, thereby offering the adult a clear enemy to reject and fight against.

The sexualized child is the figure against and through which innocence gets constructed. Adult advocates project their fantasies and nostalgia of a childhood free of conflict, polymorphous perversity, and trauma into another figure – the innocent child. She is the good object in need of protection. However, if sexualization has created a "toxic cultural environment" that is, according to feminist educator Jean Kilbourne, so pervasive that it is akin to "poisoned" air (Kilbourne, quoted in Cabrera 2007), then one must wonder, whither innocence?

The conception of the child within these two distinct figures at first appears as a defense mechanism of the paranoid schizoid type deployed to govern our discomfort. However, given the tenuous

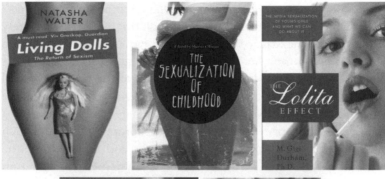

Figure 4.1 Book covers from Walter (2010), Olfman (2008), Durham (2008), Levin and Kilbourne (2008), and Oppliger (2008) emphasize the repulsion and danger associated with sexualized girlhood. All girls figured are white, scantily clad (partially unzipped and in barely-there skirts), nude, or consumed by their own gaze. Conceptualized as broken, they are visually represented in a fractured manner – exposed torso, hand holding onto a short skirt, doll over genitals and open mouthed. Ironically, these images reproduce the very representations of girlhood that the authors critique in order to sell their own messages of rescue.

Sources: Virago Press; Praeger Publishers; Gerald Duckworth & Co; Ballantine Books; McFarland & Co.

nature of innocence within these narratives, it is important to note that a paranoid schizoid defense is only part of the overall defense structure within this discourse. Innocence as the normative and ideal condition of childhood within these movements is ultimately a function of guilt and represents an adult attempt "to put the bits" of the child back together again. Although this narrative effectively annihilates the sexualized girl by casting her outside of childhood itself and prefiguring her as an object of disgust, this conception is ultimately unbearable because the ubiquity of the problem would mean that all girls should be destroyed. Reparation has to produce an object that is lovable and capable of loving – the sexually innocent girl. Innocence then operates as recompense because such vitriolic projections bring with them guilt and the need for the reparation. Ultimately, we vacillate between depressive reparation and paranoid schizoid splitting. If this is the case, what lies beneath this discourse of child protection is, in part, hatred, loathing, and repugnance. The adult preoccupation with sexual innocence defends against disgust and anxiety and thus may in fact protect the child from an unconscious longing for her annihilation and the feelings she evokes. Nevertheless, in the end, reparation does nothing for the girl deemed promiscuous – she is firmly ensconced in her position because the adult is not yet free of the repetition that led to this splitting and guilt in the first place.

Conclusion

Since the early 1800s, discourses on the sexual child (and the protection of sexual innocence) have more often than not reflected and reproduced the dominant ideals of the Anglophone West (Luker 1998; Hunt 1999; Mort 2000; Darby 2006; Egan and Hawkes 2010). In this sense, the producers of these discourses have had little trouble claiming the moral, political, and, at times, even scientific high ground in the circulation of their ideas and concomitant production of panic (Egan and Hawkes 2010). The conceptual architecture of presence and absence, compulsion, and the need for expertise require a particular picture of the childhood else such presumptions would have far less cultural traction. By tracing the psychoanalytic mechanisms at work within the most recent discourse on sexualization, we can better illuminate why such ideas are so easily reproduced and taken for granted as natural.

As I have shown, the figure of the sexual child within this discourse is an image pieced together by the fantasies, projections, and desires of adults. As such, their perception of the past (as pure and carefree and thus asexual) functions like a screen reconstruction rather than a transparent reflection. Although it is true that perfect memory is impossible, a screen reconstruction has less touch with reality because of its fantasmatic nature, and due to the fact that it is distorted by suggestions from an external source (in this case, the long history of panic surrounding childhood sexuality as well as anxieties surrounding sins of the gender and social class that I discussed in previous chapters). It is important to note that these reconstructions are not idiosyncratic; rather, their place as dominant discourse speaks to Anglophone cultural comfort with this framing. The conceptualization of childhood sexuality (as asexual and thus innocent) and the compulsive impact of sexualization is a screen reconstruction produced by adults in order to defend against the anxiety sparked by pre-Oedipal eroticism. Although we might then argue that the problem of sexualization is an adult problem rather than the child's, this discourse is dangerous because it mires the child within the thicket of adult projection, and promotes particular forms of social intervention based on this screen reconstruction. As childhood studies scholars have long pointed out, when it comes to the domain of sexuality – children have little voice in the policies and actions which shape school, medical, or governmental policy and thus are particularly subject to outside perception (Heins 2001; Levine 2002; Angelides 2004, 2008; Buckingham and Bragg 2004; Robinson 2008).

These projections about the child get reproduced with ease because there are few, if any, alternative culture conceptions to act as "reality principles" against which to judge their validity.[6] In recent history, those who produce such alternative perspectives are often cast as suspicious, uncaring, or worse, potentially deviant (Angelides 2004, 2008). Nevertheless, it is important to note that, although these conceptions of the child have a long history, they are neither monolithic nor universal. Not all cultures view the child and its sexuality in the same way, nor does the same culture unceasingly produce the same ideas about sex and childhood (i.e., both psychoanalysis and the decade of the 1970s in the Anglophone West provide striking counterexamples). Adult fantasies about the eroticism of childhood do not take place in a vacuum; rather, they are also shaped by the culture in which they are experienced. The interaction between cultural narratives and adult memories of the past are dynamically intertwined. While this interplay further illuminates that these discourses are by no means written in stone and thus that they are alterable in the future, its persistence also renders visible the tenacity (or seductive quality) of this vision of the child and its sexuality.

Conclusion:
Reflexive Reticence, Affective Response, and the Social Construction of Sexual Problems

Prelude

Imagine a slightly gawky 13-year-old girl with sandy blonde hair set in place with ample amounts of *Dep* hair gel and *Aqua Net*. If you watch for a bit you will see me, Danielle, and my best friend, Kristin, applying *Cover Girl* liquid make-up, eye liner (inside the top and bottom lid) and *Bonnie Bell* lip gloss, probably Dr. Pepper flavored, while *The Go Go's*, *Bananarama*, or *Duran Duran* plays in the background. After we finish, cast your gaze downward and you will find me on the floor peering up at Kristin while she places her feet either side of my hips and sports a slightly devious grin. She has lent me a pair of jeans that I am determined to wear. The latest trend is super tight and getting into them is a team sport. As she bends over me, my eyes come to rest on her chin and I smell her soda-flavored lips. When she bends further still, I feel the tips of her strawberry blonde hair on my nose and begin to giggle. After taking a deep breath, I say, "Okay, ready." Dressing up always involved the same ritual – after I inched her zipper up and fastened the top button, Kristin would turn her attention to me. While I can't bring to mind what brand of jeans they were on that particular night, I can remember that getting them on involved a wire hanger being hooked into the zipper toggle and Kristin pulling. On other occasions there were pliers.

The sensation that gets evoked when I think about my time with Kristin during the fall of that year is being firmly encased in something that felt good. This was the time when Brooke Shields would not let anyone come between her and her Calvin Klein jeans, and when Gloria Vanderbilt and Jordache where coveted by many of the girls in my working-class neighborhood. It was pleasurable being wrapped in that pellicle of denim that was part chastity belt (they were incredibly hard to get both on and off), part fashion statement (they were a brand of some sort), and part visual signifier in the semiotics of my desire to be desired or desirable. To be honest, a desire for the male gaze does not resonate with my recollections. It was the intimacy and ritual of getting one another into those contraptions that was so enticing. Looking back on our nights through the lens of my 40-year-old self, I am struck by the quality of our interactions which seem from the outside erotic – I am sure part of it was. However, when I reflect on the memories, feelings, and sensations of that time, it is the more sensual aspects – jeans on skin, the feel of lip gloss sticky and sweet, and the pleasure of dancing to the music, that come to the fore. I remember that the entire thing (hair, make-up, and clothes) seemed, at least in my mind, for an audience of two – we did not go to parties or get into much trouble. Mostly, we walked to our local haunt, the Baskin Robbins, got a scoop of Pink Bubblegum ice cream, strolled around the neighborhood and, on rare occasions, headed to the mall. We wanted to look good, undoubtedly, but what that meant was amorphous; I think it was some combination of rebellion, play, identification, curiosity, and desire. When I asked Kristin about her memories from this time, she laughed and said, "We were so funny," and "Do you remember our hair?!" but otherwise it was pretty unremarkable. What I am certain of is that in the maelstrom of my pre-adolescence that was dominated by an autocratic alcoholic father and my mother's palpable stress over being unable to pay the bills, my times with Kristin lip-synching to pop music, getting into skin-tight jeans, and walking down Colbath Avenue were some of the happiest.

Twenty plus years, a doctoral degree, and significantly more discretionary income later, I had a fight with my mother.

Mom: Your niece and I went to the mall today.
Danielle: Sounds like fun. What did she buy?
Mom: A couple of sweaters, some thong underwear and a pair of jeans.
Danielle: Mom! She is only 12. What were you thinking? What does she need thong underwear for? Are you keeping an eye on her?

A heated argument ensued over why my niece could possibly want a thong and what that meant. Actually, a more apt description would be that I was consumed by the question of why she would desire a thong and what the unspoken implications and impacts (behavioral, subjective, and sexual) of such a purchase were . . . consequences that I felt were being ignored. My mother, on the other hand, was quite calm and insisted that my niece just liked the way the thong fit, nothing more, nothing less. It was simply a matter of taste. Such a mundane expression seemed implausible and ultimately unsatisfying.

When we hung up, I phoned Australia. In the midst of retelling the story to my dear friend Gail, I wondered, "Why am I reacting like this?" And, "what is so dangerous about a thong?" Gail gently prodded me to think critically about these questions. Afterward, I called my niece. When I asked her, "I was thinking about buying a thong, so I was wondering, why do you like them?" Her answer was immediate and very clear, "They are more comfortable." It seemed to me that I could either listen to her or not. I could also choose to see that her choice was as complicated as mine. That such decisions are made within the complicated context of taste, fit, advertising and corporate capital, agency, group identification, biography, fantasy, history, gender, sexuality, race, religion, mood, and more mundane considerations like weather or event.

While it would be deeply irresponsible to claim that any of us can truly know and understand the vast terrain of conscious and unconscious forces of an individual and ideological nature shaping the decisions we make on an everyday basis, it would be equally erroneous to suppose that we are simply automata falling into an ideological lockstep with "the masses." Nevertheless, what I find most compelling some years later is how all my knowledge, political commitments, and personal history could be eclipsed so easily by the emotional intensity and concomitant assumptions evoked by the mix of sexuality, youth, and consumer culture that got conflated and distilled in my conception of the thong that afternoon. Almost alchemical in nature, this piece of clothing seemed capable of transforming my young niece into someone else altogether – a precocious and suspect tweenaged girl. It felt completely given that this thing – the thong – was a magical object endowed with a set of motivations and could produce potential actions that must be controlled. Given the increasingly nuanced and insidious marketing schemes, media, and advertisements using sexual images to sell products to children and adults, discomfort makes sense. And yet, this did not feel adequate because I assumed that she would become the worst part of popular culture. My discomfort and suspicion became the lens through which I viewed her purchase and informed my predictions of her future.

Attempting to tease out the fine mesh of my own projections regarding objects, affect, sexuality, and their relation to young female bodies, I wondered why it was that sexualized clothing items, even ones I could not actually see (e.g., bralettes and thongs), felt so evocative? Was it something about the object – a piece of lingerie that has been coded by culture and companies to evoke the feeling of being sexy in the body of the consumer? In part, yes. Could the thong also produce a far more complicated response in the consumer (comfort, insecurity, pleasure, embarrassment)? Sure. Can a young person feel pleasure from clothing that is not sexual but more akin to the feeling some people get from silk, cashmere, linen, and even denim? When I am not rushing, putting on a silk blouse is a glorious thing. Without denying the complexity of taste or branding, are tween and teenage girls allowed tiny pleasures which serve no other purpose but the momentary stimulation of their skin from a nice fabric? Or is this too dangerous? As

I pondered all these questions, it struck me that something far more complicated was going on.

In case the reader is wondering, my niece has very traditional views on marriage (she was married at 18 and is a stay-at-home wife), monogamy (she dated her husband long before they were married), and in her role as wife and as a future stay-at-home mother (she is hoping to get pregnant and have her first baby by 20). Hardly the wild girl depicted in the sexualization literature or in my initial reaction, but – as I have discussed throughout this book – neither are most girls.

Initially, *my preoccupations, anxieties, and conflicts* tinted my perceptions to such an extent that they momentarily limited my ability to listen to and understand my niece. It was my visceral experience that led me to think about the nature of affect in calls for sexual protection. My reaction was all the more remarkable because, in addition to forgetting my own experiences as an early adolescent, I had already conducted research and published on the history of ideas on childhood sexuality. I became fascinated by what was behind such an intense experience and how it initially obscured my perception. This piqued my curiosity and led me to explore the epistemological and historical assumptions as well as the use of affect (or emotion work) in the reports, newspaper articles, and popular books being published on the problem of sexualization.

Affect and the Construction of Social Problems

After reviewing materials (governmental documents, popular texts, blogs, newspaper articles, and reports) published over the past six years on sexualization in the United States, the United Kingdom, and Australia, I have found that although this discourse speaks to an important material conduction, an increasingly sexualized media and commodity landscape, it ultimately falls short of its stated political goals – the protection of girls. The flaw in their argument, that sexualization produces compulsive sex and pathological femininity, is dangerous because of its regulatory and normalizing impulse. The manner in which these ideas get naturalized is complicated. Promoting a hypodermic model of consumption, girls' consumption translates into sexualization; however, ignoring the vast amount of demographic and ethnographic data on girls' sexuality, media consumption, and meaning making obscures the complex ways in which girls negotiate popular culture and, equally importantly, actually behave. Popular culture is ultimately depoliticized because sexualization gets transformed into an individual psychological problem rather than a cultural issue. Its deficit model (sexualized girls are cognitively, morally, and emotionally lacking or damaged) conceptualizes sexual girls as deviant rather than focusing its attention on sexism, racism, homophobia, and classism. Within the popular literature and media, the sexualized girl is constructed as a white, heterosexual, and middle-class girl. Girls who fall outside this designation are either absent (lesbian girls and girls of color) or inferred to be part of the problem (e.g., working poor girls). In the construction of risk and outcome, this discourse draws on and reproduces longstanding middle-class fantasies of the eroticism of the poor in the service of their message. As I have illustrated, this discourse speaks to something beyond media consumption – it is a displacement for a larger set of cultural instabilities revolving around the economy, the family, the nation, and, for some, the future of feminism itself. Finally, reproducing longstanding cultural fears of the child and its sexuality, this discourse splits the girl into sexualized and innocent in order to manage disgust, shame, and discomfort. Affect is central to the way in which these assumptions get naturalized and taken for granted as truthful. Consequently, the sexualized girl is a symptom of cultural instability and adult preoccupation more than it is an accurate description of the complicated project of growing-up girl.

I hope that my analysis has illuminated why conceptual clarity, empirical grounding, historical awareness, and exploring the way in which a topic affects us are crucial to knowledge construction, particularly when we are making claims about social problems and crafting policies of protection.[1] Writing from the position of our affective experiences instead of interrogating the density of experience within which girls relate to, embody, or live with media puts us at risk of getting mired in the realm of projection or displacement. When this happens, our understanding of girls gets refracted through the prism of adult presumptions, preoccupations, and affective states such as loathing, love, desire, fixation, and fascination. In the end, we may demonize, exoticize, or canonize the girl – in some literature she is only a victim, in others only an agentic warrior – either way, she becomes a figure frozen in the amber of adult projection.

This does not mean that authors are delusional or that sexualization is a fantasy. It is undoubtedly the case that corporations rely upon and reproduce sexist, racist, and homophobic images of young people to sell products and create brand loyalty. We continue to live in a culture where the sexuality of girls and women is too often the ground upon which conservative politics get played out. During the writing of this conclusion, this was made painfully clear with the Republican presidential candidate Mitt Romney's vow to do away with funding for Planned Parenthood – a bombastic claim used, at least in part, to bolster his assertion that he is a "true conservative" (Min Kim 2012). This comment also took place during a week when Arizona passed a bill that allowed employers to deny birth control for female employees unless they get a note from their doctor proving that they require the prescription for health reasons (Dalven 2012). It is also the case that our fragmented and hyper-mediated culture is impacting both community and the individual in deeply complicated ways (Pfohl 1992; Bauman 2000; Zizek 2009; Grossberg 2010; Goldman and Papson 2011). Notwithstanding, all of this gets distilled into pathology instead of politics in the sexualization literature. This makes sense for conservative authors writing on the topic. Such a vision may help adults feel better, but I fear it does little for girls – particularly those deemed sexualized and deficient. In the end, it is distracting for feminism – by reproducing part of our more problematic past and getting mired in pathological prognosis, we lose sight of far more pressing issues such as poverty, globalization, workplace harassment, and disparities in health care.

The sexualized girl is a metaphor for our cultural condition. She represents the erosion (or perceived erosion) of the family, nation, class stability, identity politics, and the distinction between adult and child. For this reason, she is deeply important, she becomes the repository for cultural discontent, anxiety, hope, fascination, and frustration, as well as the collective disgust, rage, and shame many feel about the culture at large. Fighting against her corruption helps allay feelings of helplessness, fear, and rage. She provides a platform to reinvigorate a particular vision of the future for conservatives and re-legitimates the vision and voice of a particular subset of feminist activists. While it may help momentarily discharge the impotence of living in an increasingly alienating, confusing, and fragmented culture, it does little for those who get marginalized as a result. Within popular literature, only certain girls seem worthy of care and protection (white, middle-class, and heterosexual), while others get constructed as either unimportant (queer girls) or, worse, come to serve as cautionary tales (working-class girls, girls who are sexual, and girls of color) and examples of what "good" girls don't do.

How can we decipher whether our thinking is moving in this direction? Not very easily, but I think a first step might be to attend to the following. First, critically examine how the "problem" is constructed. Analyze data from multiple sources and disciplines. Trace the epistemological, empirical, and historical assumptions as well as the way in which affect is being deployed in the construction of a social problem to see whether it is working in a metaphorical or decontextualized manner. Second, explore who is being constructed as problematic and/or endangered. If certain groups are being ignored or marginalized, attempt to figure out why. Is it because the problem really only is gender, race, class, or sexually specific, or is something else going on? Is this problem driven more by emotional pleas or data? Third, examine history. Where is the problem coming from? How is it similar to or different from movements of the past? Finally, follow the affect. What are you feeling about the topic? Where might this be coming from? Use affect instructively as both a window into an issue and an avenue for understanding where your feelings about something begin and end. This is by no means an exhaustive list, more of a first step.

Donna Haraway highlights how knowledge production is always situated (Haraway 1990). Our location in the world shapes how we perceive it and thus it demands that we account for this in our research and take a careful and ethical approach. Haraway argues that a situated understanding requires "that the object of knowledge be pictured as an actor and agent, not a screen or a ground or a resource, never finally as slave to the master that closes off the dialectic in his unique agency and authorship of 'objective knowledge'" (Haraway 1990: 197). Taking into account "the agency" of the people or phenomenon we study "transforms the entire project of producing social theory" (Haraway 1990: 197). Avoiding "false knowledge" comes from "granting the status of agent/actor to the 'objects'" to the world we study in both the social and natural sciences (Haraway 1990: 197). Thinking critically about our affective and visceral reactions about sexualization is one way to grant the status of sexual citizenship to young people.

Does this mean we try to do away with emotion and affect in our politics and research? Absolutely not! I do not even think it is possible. Issues that compel us, research questions we want to pursue, the theoretical perspectives we are resonant with are not random; they are ignited by something deeply personal, but not necessarily straightforward or fully understood at the outset. As Elspeth Probyn notes, "we work ideas through our bodies; we write and write about society not as an abstraction but as composed of actual bodies in proximity" and recognizing what you are trying to do or evoke in the reader (Probyn 2010: 76). Accordingly, "the body of the writer becomes the battleground where ideas and experiences collide, sometimes to produce new visions of life" precisely because the affective is at work in the writing process – it compels us, arrests us, and makes the attempts to reach the reader in our writing a source of anxiety and desire (Probyn 2010: 89).[2]

Interrogating one's own position (as well as employing a systematic method) in our construction of social life helps us explore the way in which our writing is situated politically, ethically, and corporeally. Feminist theorist and psychoanalyst Jessica Benjamin argues that our preoccupations, fixations, conflicts, insecurities, character, and culture often impinge upon the way in which we see the other in our everyday lives (Benjamin 1998). Working to acknowledge the other and grant recognition is an ethical and political act that comes with practice and reflexivity. Taking this idea seriously may help us gain a better sense of ourselves as researchers and activists, and, equally important, it can further enrich the concept of positionality by asking us to be reflexive about our own affective reactions and responses in the doing of social research. Exploring our own reactions might help give us a better understanding of just what it is that we are actually writing about – whether it is about the espoused topic or a displacement that may be obscuring something far more unsettling.

When crafting research about another, and particularly when it is crafted for someone's "own good," we need to attend to the "covert, scarcely visible, yet persistent reactions that pervade" listening and responding (Jacobs 1986: 296).[3] This does not mean that our research should be a chronicle of narcissistic responses, but rather that a more reflexive humility should guide our production of social problems in the hope of crafting a more nuanced under-standing of girls and the deeply complicated contexts within which they make decisions about life in general.

Notes

Introduction: Sexualization as a Social Problem

1 Discourses are social creations and thus function as social objects –
they are things in themselves. They emerge in particular historical
moments and are used as truth regimes to explain the nature of things,
groups, or events in the world around us. As Foucault illustrates, they
emerge from particular institutions and can often, although by no
means always, function as a dominant form of knowledge that shapes
particular social endeavors. To this end, discourses are neither neutral
nor ephemeral; they work to legitimate a particular vision of the
world and the institutions that are said to be crucial for its functioning (Foucault 1980). Discourses, however, are never unitary – the
manner in which they are interpolated and lived varies (however,
there are patterns, and discourses do not produce endless idiosyncratic
responses), and resistance to them is a natural outcome. They produce
cultural ideals of morality, righteousness, normality, ethics, and justify
things such as war or the death penalty. They also produce anti-war
movements and movements such as surrealism. Because they function
as regimes of truth into the nature of things, they are external objects
that often go unnoticed and come to be seen as if natural (Foucault

1980). Although most poststructuralists view discourses as a structural manifestation which explains the power and knowledge at work in the creation of particular ideas, this perspective cannot help articulate why certain discourses resonate more strongly than others and "just *feel* right" to a particular individual or group of individuals.

2 As with most ideas on sexuality, cultural values ebb and flow at various periods, and ideas about the sexual child are no different. For example, the assumptions at work in the discursive production of the sexual child from the 1970s stand in stark contrast to most contemporary narratives on the child and its sexuality (Martinson 1994; Angelides 2004). However, the modern history of ideas on childhood sexuality is distinct in that it is more often than not plagued by fear, projection, fascination, and consternation. As historians and childhood studies scholars have illustrated, the history of the sexual child differs from other populations deemed sexually deviant or in need of sexual protection because of Anglophone conceptions of childhood (Males 1996; Angelides 2004; Darby 2005; Robinson and Davies 2008; Romesberg 2008; Egan and Hawkes 2010; Faulkner 2010). Ideally, childhood as a cultural category is constructed as mutually exclusive and distinct from adulthood. Although this conception of the child is a fairly recent phenomenon, its deployment has been shaped in distinct ways according to race, class, and gender (Swain and Howe 1995; Sanchez-Eppler 2005; Cunningham 2006; Fass 2006; Bernstein 2011). For example, the belief in the sentimental quality of childhood is not a transhistorical phenomenon. Rather, its emergence is linked to a particular socio-historical context – as children were deemed to be less useful contributors to the familial economy, their value as sentimental objects in the family rose (Zelizer 1985).

Sentimentalization was further complicated as it extended beyond the middle-class conception of the child to poor and immigrant children, because it was used as a barometer against which to judge and render suspect poor and immigrant families and, in so doing, justified surveillance and entrée into families by various social institutions (e.g., public health and social work). However, the "harm of labor" in the lives of children seems only to apply to children in urban settings or to work differently in rural contexts where farm work has been a central feature of life, but one that falls outside the concept of child labor (Gordon 1999). Nevertheless, while childhood as a category is deeply complex and often varied, there is a strong cultural attachment to maintaining its difference from adulthood.

Most dominant discourses that have emerged within the Anglophone West (Freudian psychoanalysis notwithstanding) have, on the surface, conceptualized childhood as antithetical to sexual emergence (however, this tends to primarily apply to white upper-middle-class children) – to be sexual is to be adult; the emergence of eroticism is seen as abhorrent and thus evidence of pathology (medical, moral, or psychological) or evidence of outside intervention (from an adult or other corrupt social force) (Foucault 1980). This vision nullifies the child as a sexual citizen because the child is inherently incapable of making meaning of or articulating rights regarding sexuality. Notwithstanding the vigorous discourses surrounding the boundary between the child and the adult as well as the need to defend its asexual and innocent nature, it is equally the case that the dividing line between these states is always already fragile and under threat and thus in need of measures to insure its stability. To this end, the innocent or sexually endangered child is more often than not constructed against its socially sanctioned counterpart, the erotic or sexually knowing child.

The persistence of these anxieties may speak to the fact that Anglophone culture is as engrossed by the figure of the sexually corrupted child as it is to its innocent counterpart. Both operate as a barometer of social decay or progress, as a nostalgic longing for a pure past, a signal of impending societal doom or as a utopian possibility for reshaping the future as well as a site for social intervention; nevertheless, both figures are, to use historian Robin Bernstein's term, "imagined" children in that they are symbolic figures as opposed to material actors (Bernstein 2011). Fears regarding sexual corruption from a variety of sexually salacious sources (comic books, television, rap music, the Internet, clothing, etc.) or deviant populations (immigrants, the poor, gays and lesbians, or the pedophile) tend to gain momentum during times of social upheaval or crisis. As my research with Gail Hawkes illustrated, the imperiled child historically served as a proxy for cultural discontent and the desire to manage larger social ills (Egan and Hawkes 2010). To this end, the discourse on sexualization is situated within a larger socio-historical context that has been strikingly persistent over the last two centuries (Foucault 1980; Hunt 1999; Mort 2000; Furedi 2002; Egan and Hawkes 2010; Faulkner 2010; Bernstein 2011; Hawkes and Egan 2012).

3 In popular manuals or news stories on the topic, a parent's response to sexualization is also reduced to a singular viable response – that girls must be saved from a sexualized childhood and a future of self-destructive behavior, or you will lose them altogether. Any other perspective is deemed irresponsible or as evidence of bad parenting (Press Association 2003; Reist 2009a, 2009b; Carey 2011). As qualitative research from Britain recently revealed, parents express a variety of thoughtful responses toward sexualized cultural representations, and the actions they take for the sake of their children are dynamic and often involve good conversations with their children (Bragg 2012a, 2012b). As I will illustrate in chapter 1, research reveals that children and adults have a far more nuanced relationship with cultural commodities than the deterministic equation offered in the popular sexualization literature.

4 These repetitions continue unless or until the original conflict gets worked through. The point of analysis is to help the analysand uncover these conflicts so that she or he may live a more free life.

5 Michel Foucault argues that the modern conception of sexuality was a pivotal point in the shift from the ancient regime to biopower. Unlike previous forms of governmentality, which had power over life, biopower brings "life and its mechanism into the realm of explicit calculations and made knowledge-power an agent of transformation of human life" (Foucault 1980: 143). Through the surveillance of sex, a proliferation of technologies invested "the body, health, modes of subsistence and habituation, living conditions, the whole space of existence" (Foucault 1980: 144).

Chapter 1: What is Sexualization?

1 Clearly, the goal of ending sexual exploitation of women is an important one; however, the construction of the crisis and proposed solutions are created without consulting groups they are attempting

to "rescue," and without a systematic understanding of cultural and individual context (Agustin 2007).

2 A more current example can be found in a recent Opinion Editorial in the British newspaper *The Guardian*. Gail Dines and Julia Long state that radical feminists are not engaging in moral panic or moral politics in discussions of sexualization. Rather, they assert that their primary political goal is to stem the tide of sexualized representations by "the corporate-controlled media industry that mass produces these images" (Dines and Long 2011). This assertion resonates with and speaks to a larger feminist critique of sexist, racist, and homophobic representations; however, their claims become more problematic when they depart from media criticism and objectification and move towards the pathologization of girls. Dines and Long revert to a psychological discourse in their statement that media damages the "cognitive functioning, physical and mental health, sexuality, and attitudes and beliefs" of girls (APA report quoted in Dines and Long 2011). Ironically, this Opinion Editorial was written in the midst of the *Pornified? Complicating Debates about the Sexualisation of Culture* conference, which both Dines and Long attended, a conference which featured empirical work from international scholars that challenged binary and reductionist assertions. Unfortunately, none of the research from other feminist scholars at the conference was taken into account. A deficit model of girlhood gets promoted in declarations which reduce the consumption of popular culture to a causal outcome of "risky sexual behaviour, higher rates of eating disorders, depression and low self-esteem, and reduced academic performance" to the exclusion of other findings (Dines and Long 2011). While I agree with Dines and Long that their argument should not be dismissed, out of hand, as simply "moral panic" or moral politics (it is far more complicated), I would, however, note that the way in which they draw causal conclusions, pathologize girls, and deploy affect in their calls for reformation is not all that different from their conservative counterparts.

3 An exception to this rule is psychologist Sharon Lamb who is currently undertaking research on sexualization and has written about the need for empirical substantiation for the claims being made about sexualization (Lamb 2001).

4 The report for the Labour government was written by a

"celebrity" psychologist, Linda Papadopoulos (contributor to Australia's *Cosmopolitan* and the psychologist for the British version of the reality show *Big Brother*). Reg Baily, head of the conservative Mother's Union, wrote the report for the Cameron government. Neither are experts on the topic.

Chapter 2: (Hetero)Sexualization, Pathological Femininity, and Hope for the Future

1 To be clear, he is not referring to trans youth or the queering of gender; rather, he is making reference to the celebration of girls who act as crass and rowdy as boys.

2 The Nielsen company collects data on television viewership in the United States.

3 Fan culture also spans a wide variety of contexts; for example, girls may identify with Italian tennis star Francesca Schiavone, WNBA star Rebekkah Brunson, and Miley Cyrus as much as they might like Gossip Girl, Christian Rock or the X games. Moreover, girls can identify with a celebrity on one level (as musicians) and reject them on another (as sexual subjects). For example, Sue Jackson's research with girls in New Zealand illustrates the fickle nature of fandom when it comes to sexual transgressions – girls she interviewed spurned Miley Cyrus when she appeared nude on the cover of *Vanity Fair* (Jackson 2011; see also Buckingham and Bragg 2004). Girls are not passive consumers, neither are they free agents – their tastes, values, and consumption are often complicated, intricate, and, at times, contradictory. Emma Renold's and Jessica Ringrose's case studies on girls' use of sexualized symbols such as the Playboy bunny on social networking sites reveal just how complicated their use can be – girls felt pressured and resisted, at times they felt defiant, and at others defeated (Renold and Ringrose 2011a).

4 Please see Spark a Movement at www.sparksummit.com for an excellent example.

5 This video spurred a media firestorm. There is debate over whether Jonah is gay – something, I think, that is irrelevant because if he was bullied because of the perception that he was gay that too is homophobic. What was more remarkable was the host of videos posted

in response from young men and women of their stories and their support.

6 http://www.youtube.com/watch?v=SXH2K7OC37s; http://www.youtube.com/watch?v=tRXjqpfOnS0; http://www.youtube.com/watch?v=R-huPai1Srk&feature=related; http://www.youtube.com/watch?v=PFVvBgLjnW8&feature=related; http://www.youtube.com/watch?v=MraMVmQ-xD0&feature=related; http://www.youtube.com/watch?v=EQXboElx_V8; http://www.youtube.com/watch?v=6pnlrBhxReM; http://www.youtube.com/watch?v=Vy9vM15OMVc&feature=related; http://www.youtube.com/watch?v=2TK02tMOp_g&feature=related; http://www.youtube.com/watch?v=Cc223-FFZrI&feature=related (all accessed January 29, 2012).

7 www.sparksummit.com

8 www.sparksummit.com

9 Essentialism presumes that there are inherent differences in the sexual nature of men and women (their sexuality is mutually exclusive due to its biological basis), and when there is a violation on either side, pathology is presumed. For an excellent review of the problems with this form of logic, see Weeks (2009).

10 In discussions of sexualization, the wide terrain of sexuality in the lives of girls gets distilled into experiences of sexual violence. It is politically crucial for feminists to confront and fight sexual violence on every front; but I also believe that our thinking about girls and sexuality should not stop there.

11 It is also worth noting that although sexualization of heterosexual boys is not a popular topic, our culture is far from comfortable with the current state of boyhood. In fact, concerns and anxieties regarding boyhood have also catalyzed a genre of self-help books and parenting manuals. In many of these texts, it is not a boy's sexuality but his gender that is the problem. Bullying, lack of ambition, hopelessness, dangerous and self-destructive behavior, low school performance, or violence are considered far more dire and are said to stem from media, computer addiction, a dearth of good role models, and boredom more than the reception of erotic materials (Sax 2009; Tyre 2009; Young and Young 2010; Hamilton 2011). It is beyond the scope of this book to analyze these claims for accuracy, but it is important to

note that similar rhetorical devices (affect, hyperbole, and a narrow conception of boyhood) are employed in the service of the message.

In more conservative tomes, males are confused, feckless, and emasculated because they have lost their (natural) place as the authoritative leader in the heterosexual dyad and in society at large (Dalton 2005). The "crisis" is that masculine supremacy is under threat (we need to help create "real men") and needs to be reinstalled (Sax 2009; Young and Young 2010). In other manuals, it is a boy's lack of achievement or violence and self-defeatism that poses the greatest risk (Tyre 2009; Hamilton 2011). Within both, the issue is that boys are not cultivating the right kind of masculinity (it is either not enough or too much). Conservative authors believe that our culture has devalued heterosexual masculinity to such an extent that boys have become aimless and confused.

Imperiled boyhood is believed to come from another source – violent media and video games, social networking sites or the "addiction to the Internet," drugs, and alcohol, which all seem to pose a far greater threat to heterosexual boys than the erotic (Kindlon and Thompson 2000; Biddulph 2008; Sax 2009; Tyre 2009; Hamilton 2011). Reviewing Maggie Hamilton's bibliography for her chapter on sexualization reveals that her sources are, with the exception of one, all dealing with girls – whereas other chapters such as "losing tweens to virtual worlds" or "the bullying thing" or any other have numerous citations on boys.

12 The lack of concern regarding boyhood within most of the literature is remarkable. During the writing of this chapter, only one book on the topic of sexualized boyhood was published in Australia: *What's Happening to Our Boys?* by Maggie Hamilton – however, unlike all the other popular texts on sexualization that have been available in simultaneous release across the Anglophone West, this text was not available (nor was there a forthcoming publication date) in the United Kingdom or the United States (Hamilton 2011).

13 This raises interesting questions about whether discussions of self-sexualization may have an unintended consequence – do girls who seek out self-objectification or in Farley's term prostitution behaviors become less deserving of empathy if raped? Boys cannot want to be objects and girls must pay if they revel in this status.

14 Within this context, innocence was linked to a state of "holy ignorance" and therefore seemed to eclipse social categories of class,
gender, and race – as Bernstein illustrates, children were indeed
classed, raced, and gendered, but to be innocent in the nineteenth century was about "the performance of not-noticing, a per-
formed claim of slipping beyond social categories" (Bernstein 2011).
Bernstein argues that the character little Eve in the Uncle Tom story
is emblematic of this cultural system.

15 As a result, for Americans this production of "holy ignorance" helped
legitimate whiteness and racial difference as the category against
which whiteness was produced. This binary "understanding race in
terms of white and non-white, or a 'black and white' polarization
that erases nonblack people of color – gained legibility through nineteenth century childhood" (Bernstein 2011). To this end, childhood
innocence functioned as "the perfect alibi" because of its ability to
"remember while appearing to forget, but more importantly, the
production of racial memory through forgetting" (Bernstein 2011: 8).

16 As I detail in chapter 4, it is my contention that within the sexualization literature, innocence is secondary and is the result of guilt, at base
a reaction formation to disgust and possibly even titillation.

Chapter 3: Sexualized Tastes, Middle-Class Fantasies, and Fears of Class Contagion

1 The vast terrain of literature on the intersection of taste, manners,
social structure, and identity is far too broad, rich, and varied to
address in this chapter.

2 The rise of medicalization in the hygiene movement created a
context where male doctors sought to usurp the authority of women
to create expert advice on child rearing.

3 For Moses, the answer is located in generations past – specifically, in
the "feminist, post feminist and post pill generation" (Moses 2011).
Unlike the women who came before them, girls growing up in the
1960s, 1970s, and 1980s were pressured to achieve womanhood "in
the bedroom" (Moses 2011). Ironically, then, Moses argues that the
movement which sought to promote women's rights and end sexual
violence also promoted promiscuity. In the final analysis, we are told

that the women's movement unwittingly created a new breed of ambivalent mothers stymied by the sexualization of their own girls.

4 What remains fuzzy in this popular article (it had over 600 hits in the first two days and as a result several radio interviews with the author) is where this information on girls comes from (other than her experience as a mother and friend) and how maternal shame translates into purchasing school clothes fit for "a prostitute;" nevertheless, Moses' message to mothers is unequivocal. Although the young male sex drive and its need for discharge remains unquestioned and thus naturalized throughout, Moses is quick to caution against perpetuating a double standard and advises against the use of condemnation (Moses 2011; Moses, in Martin 2011). However, what this might look like becomes confused at best, when reading statements such as, "if you're the campus mattress, chances are that you need therapy more than you need condemnation" (Moses 2011).

5 Many feminist and postcolonial critics have pointed out that projection is also a common facet of our cultural imaginary (Benjamin 1988; Fuss 1995; Butler 2004; Fanon 2008). Franz Fanon highlights the gravity of projection in his writing on the colonial project (Fanon 2008). As his writings painfully illustrate, all of the qualities the French felt were loathsome, disgusting, or repulsive were projected onto the colonized; as a result, the colonized became all body, only body, orifice, and animal. This production of the other in only corporeal terms fostered the "epidermalization of race," whereby interiority, ego, and rationality were evacuated from the colonized and as a result created one of the central justifications (we must save them from their wanton ways) for the colonial project (Fanon 2008). Projection is produced in tandem with, and reproduces, power and carries with it a social and individual history.

6 In this sense, influence and identification translate into metamorphosis and, once erected, barriers of moral values and respectability erode upon contact. A self-perpetuating system, girls are infected, engage in sexualized behaviors, and thus infect others – what is important to note is that, unlike feminist anti-pornography narratives from the 1970s and 1980s where women and girls were considered objectified and thus victims of the patriarchal gaze, sexualization narratives add a psychological dimension – the production of pathological subjectivity

and as a result pathological behavior (MacKinnon 1988; Dworkin 2006; Dines 2011). Whereas in the past discussions of objectification focused on the structures of patriarchy and cultural change, Linda Duits and Liesbet van Zoonen note that the new discourse on sexualization is more psychological, individualized, fear based, and thus less political in its focus (Duits and van Zoonen 2011). In their critique of the Conservative government's Bailey Report, Meg Barker and Robbie Duschinsky argue that the discourse on sexualization rests upon and reproduces a neoliberal conception which erases inequality (cultural, material, and sexual) to render the problem one of "individual pathology and irresponsibility – or else the actions of a child" (Barker and Duschinsky 2012; see also Renold and Ringrose 2011a; Ringrose 2013). What is important to note is that in both of these critiques, the problem of sexualization is an individual one – and thus, the solution is cure as opposed to cultural transformation.

7 As Gail Hawkes and I, as well as many childhood studies scholars and historians, have noted, the production of innocence is also a classification that is as weighted down with desire projection and, as James Kincaid illustrates, desire, as its Janus face – sexualization (Kincaid 1992, 1998; Angelides 2004; Jenkins 2004; Robinson 2008; Robinson and Davies 2008; Egan and Hawkes 2010).

8 The extent to which concerns regarding the child and its sexuality have served as a stand-in for a broader sense of cultural insecurity in the modern period is well documented in my research with Gail Hawkes (Egan and Hawkes 2007, 2009, 2010). My analysis throughout this chapter has attempted to address how both forms are at work in ways in which class anxieties get displaced onto taste and comportment which in turn get projected onto the working-class girl.

Chapter 4: Unmanageable Bodies, Adult Disgust, and the Demand for Innocence

1 It is important to note that Freud's thesis on sexuality shifted in his early clinical work, as many of Freud's female patients spoke of being "seduced by adults or other children" at an early age (1905b: 4). In response, Freud forwarded his, now infamous, seduction

theory which states that repressed sexual trauma in childhood produces hysteria and obsessional neurosis later in life (1906). Neurotic symptoms would take place in adolescence after a relatively minor (often romantic) event triggers the memory of the original trauma (1906). However, after seeing more patients and listening to their stories, Freud rejected the theory of seduction and replaced it with a theoretical matrix that comprised fantasy, infantile sexuality, and repression. In "My views on the part played by sexuality in the aetiology of the neuroses," Freud notes that he "overestimated" the frequency "of these occurrences" and as a result was unable to "discriminate between the deceptive memories of hysterics concerning their childhood and the memory traces of actual happenings" (1905b: 4). Freud's analysis of neuroses evolved into an examination of how patients employed seduction fantasies as a defense mechanism to distance themselves from "the sexual activities" they practiced in their childhood (1905b: 4).

2 One might also posit that Freud's ideas, written over a century ago, are a relic – a proverbial fly in the amber of time past or proof positive that his theories about the sexual instinct and society were erroneous. Worse still, one might charge that the culture of sexualization is what happens when one lets the proverbial genie (libido) out of the bottle and as such sexual repression is both necessary and highly beneficial. However, Freud's emphasis on the necessity for redirecting a certain quantity of our libido, or sexual energy, toward the creation of art, new discoveries, the building of society – what he termed sublimation – renders this interpretation of his work problematic as well. Freud postulated that the tempering of sexual instincts toward less narcissistic and more socially oriented forms was part and parcel of maturation – even though this outcome was far from guaranteed (Freud 1924/1997, 1905b). To this end, Freud was neither a sexual conservative nor a sexual libertarian (Chodorow 2000).

3 It is important to note the scope of the movement against sexualization. Concerns expressed over sexualization and its outcomes have been the focus of three governmental reports in Scotland, England, and Australia (two of which found insufficient proof to support advocates' requests for policy action), a non-peer-reviewed task force of the American Psychological Association, numerous television shows,

blogs, and magazine articles. Activists from the feminist left to the deeply conservative and very religious right both lament the influence of sexualizing images and actions.

4 The sexualized girl is an evocative figure in our cultural imaginary and has been, in one guise or another, for a very long time (Egan and Hawkes 2010). She is a composite of various preoccupations and anxieties regarding gender, sexuality, race, and class within the Anglophone West and is a steadfast object of disdain in times of cultural insecurity.

5 The insights of Freud in conjunction with the transference she saw develop during play therapy provided Melanie Klein with tools for understanding the pre-Oedipal period and its persistence in adult life. Klein argues that from birth "the infant has an innate unconscious awareness of the existence of the mother" as well as a constitutional inclination toward particular destructive and libidinal tendencies (Klein 1959: 248). Accordingly, there is an innate connection to the object which is guided by somatic impulses, unconscious fantasies, and both the "libidinal and aggressive" drives (Klein 1952: 62). Klein and some of her followers depart from the classical Freudian defini- tion of instinct as autoerotic discharge based on pleasure and unpleas- ure (Grotstein 1980). According to James Grotstein, for Kleinians instincts are "always object-seeking primarily in the nutritive mode," which represents a "holistic urge [as opposed to a sexual one] or need on the part of the whole infant" (Grotstein 1980: 378–9). This holistic urge is informed by Freud's later thinking on dual drives and encompasses both the life and death instinct (Freud 1920).

After birth "the newborn baby experiences, both in the process of birth and in the adjustment to the post-natal situation, anxiety of a persecutory nature" (Klein 1959: 248). It is the death drive or "death instinct" which produces the infantile "fear of annihilation" and thus is the driving force at work in persecutory anxiety (Klein 1952: 61). Both libidinal and destructive impulses are present at birth; however, anxiety predominates. If it becomes too strong, an infant can lose interest in feeding, refuse to latch, experience deep distress and even death. A good mother helps strengthen libidinal impulses with love and understanding. However, inevitable privations are also part of life. When the infant is faced with hunger or pain and is unable to ameliorate them, persecutory anxiety and fears of annihilation bring forward splitting as a mode of defense; as such, the ego from birth onward "has the important task of defending itself against anxiety stirred up by the struggle within and by influences without" (Klein 1959: 249). The mother is "the whole of the external world" to the child during the first few months of life; "both good and bad come in his mind from her, and this leads to a twofold attitude toward the mother even under the best possible conditions" (Klein 1959: 248). In this regard, the infant's first (part) object relation is made meaningful, or in Grotstein's words an "instinctual narrative," by both oral libidinal and oral destructive impulses (Grotstein 1980). Defending against this during the paranoid schizoid phrase or position requires introjection and projection as well as splitting to "divide impulses and objects" (Klein 1959: 250).

Introjection and projection function from birth onward as some of the earliest functions of the ego (Klein 1959). To this end, "introjection means that the outer world, its impact, the situation the infant lives through, and the objects he encounters, are not only experienced as external but are taken into the self and become parts of his inner life" (Klein 1959: 250). Introjection is a continual process in both childhood and adulthood. Projection takes place simultaneously and reveals the child's capacity to "attribute to other people around him feelings of various kinds, predominately love and hate" (Klein 1959: 250). Introjection and projection are crucial to maturation and, when they are in optimal balance, normal development is likely to take place (Klein 1946, 1952). In earliest life, what gets projected and introjected are fantasies of the (part) object. As Klein states, "from one angle the processes of projection and introjections that I have been describing have to be considered as unconscious phantasies" (Klein 1959, 252). The relation between instinct and fantasy is how splitting takes place.

Susan Isaacs renders visible this connection when she argues:

> Phantasy is the mental corollary, the physic representative of instinct. There is no impulse, no instinctual urge or response which is not experienced as unconscious phantasy ... A phantasy represents the particular content of the urges or feelings

(for example, wishes, fears, anxieties, triumphs, love or sorrow) dominating the mind at the moment" (Isaacs 1952: 82).

In his exegesis on the conceptualization of instinct and fantasy in the Kleinian paradigm, Grotstein argues that "instinctual impulses are experienced *a priori* as fantasies" and thus as "primitive narratives" (Grotstein 1980: 384). Splitting and projective identification "render all perceptions into 'instinctual stories' which are split off likenesses of the self or components of the self" (Grotstein 1980: 384). Hunger or satiation is only made meaningful through its referent – the breast.

In "Notes on some schizoid mechanisms," Klein posits that "frustrations of bodily needs" are experienced as terrifying – so much so that they must be projected into an external part object and felt to be caused by them (Klein 1946: 5). The interplay of the good and bad breast is illustrated most powerfully in hallucinatory gratification or unconscious fantasies which emerge during deprivation. With frustration, the infant engages in "two interrelated processes . . . the omnipotent conjuring up of the idea object and situation, and the equally omnipotent annihilation of the bad persecutory object and the painful situation" (Klein 1946: 5). Both involve the splitting of the object and the ego into bits. Frustration produces oral sadistic and "cannibalistic" fantasies which get projected into the bad breast that must be destroyed or torn to bits and as such comes to be experienced as attacking and persecutory; the good bits are idealized as benevolent and all giving – this exaggerated idealization safeguards against persecutory anxiety.

6   It also may provide a clue as to why people were and still are reactive toward the Freudian child.

Conclusion: *Reflexive Reticence, Affective Response, and the Social Construction of Sexual Problems*

1   Few feminist theorists are as successful as Audre Lorde in illuminating the importance of emotion in the production of social change and in the formation of knowledge (Lorde 2007). The evocative nature of Lorde's work is demonstrated in her ability to capture how the uses of emotions such as anger and the erotic are crucial to survival and

the promotion of social change within a broader landscape of racism, sexism, and homophobia, as well as within the feminist movement (Lorde 2007). In her essay entitled "The uses of anger," Lorde draws on her experiences of exclusion and racism within feminist circles and the anger it inspired to fuel feminist dialogue and reflexivity (Lorde 2007). What is striking, however, is how Lorde's political use of emotion functions as a resource for the individual and a movement, but it is not used as a lens through which to construct the other. Although this essay differs from much recent literature on affect, it speaks to the power of harnessing emotion for social transformation in a way that is mindful of difference and reflexive regarding power and the seduction of marginalization.

2 Drawing on writers as far-ranging as Stephen King, Primo Levi, and Gilles Deleuze, she argues that taking the responsibility of writing and evoking a response in the reader is ethically imperative. She contends "writing is interested; it is deeply embedded in contexts, politics and bodies" (Probyn 2010: 89). In this sense, "the blush of having failed to connect with readers should compel any writer to return to the page with renewed desire to do better . . . in this task of communicating" (Probyn 2010: 89). Taking Probyn's compelling and provocative statements seriously places my research in an interesting bind precisely because most of the authors writing on sexualization are incredibly adept at spurring emotion in the reader. Moreover, it would be dishonest to claim that their writing did not come from their desire for social transformation. In this way, they have neither failed in the task of communication, nor have they shied away from embedding politics and the body in their writing. However, they have done so by stirring up trenchant Anglophone fears and rendering pathological a particular vision of girlhood. Apart from the discourse on sexualization, one can see how effective particular types of political writing and speech are at spurring the affective in the face of the material – the level of rage at work in populism offers a striking example.

3 Although Jacobs is writing about the analytic encounter – when the analyst is unable to hear and be open to the feelings of the analysand due to what he terms countertransference enactment – I believe his insights are very relevant to cultural research.

References

30isthenewblack (2011) The rise and rise of porn chic on Facebook, May 22. Available at: http://30isthenewblack.com/2010/05/22/the-rise-and-rise-of-porn-chic-on-facebook/ (accessed August 9, 2011).

Adalian, J. (2012) The 2011–12 TV Season: What we watched and what we skipped. *Vulture*, June 21. Available at: http://www.vulture.com/2012/06/201112-tv-season-by-the-numbers.html (accessed July 5, 2012).

Agustin, L.M. (2007) *Sex at the Margins: Migration, Labour Markets and the Rescue Industry*. London: Zed.

Allen, L. (2005) *Sexual Subjects: Young People, Sexuality and Education*. London: Palgrave Macmillan.

American Psychological Association (APA) (2007) Report of the APA Task Force on the sexualization of girls. American Psychological Association. Available at: http://www.apa.org/pi/wpo/sexualization.html (accessed April 25, 2008).

Anderson, W. (2006) *The Cultivation of Whiteness: Science, Health and Racial Destiny in Australia*. Durham, NC: Duke University Press.

Andrews, C.R. (2011) Rihanna and the rise of raunch pop. *The Guardian*, May 12. Available at: http://www.guardian.co.uk/music/2011/may/12/rihanna-raunch-pop (accessed May 13, 2011).

Angelides, S. (2004) Feminism, child sexual abuse and the erasure of childhood sexuality. *Gay and Lesbian Quarterly* 10.2, 141–77.

Angelides, S. (2008) Sexual offences against "children" and the question of judicial gender bias. *Australian Feminist Studies* 23.57, 359–73.

ANRED (2008) Eating Disorder Statistics. Available at: www.anred.com/stats.html (accessed February 2, 2011).

Arthur, R. (1903) *The Choice: A Purity Booklet for Young Men*. Sydney, NSW: William Brooks, Educational Printers.

Asma, S.A. (2009) *On Monsters: An Unnatural History of Our Worst Fears*. New York: Oxford University Press.

Attwood, F. (2006) Sexed up: Theorizing the sexualization of culture. *Sexualities* 8.5, 77–94.

Attwood, F. (2009) Introduction: The sexualization of culture. In: F. Attwood (ed.) *Mainstreaming Sex: The Sexualization of Western Culture*. London: IB Tauris, xxii–1.

Attwood, F. (2011) *OnScenity*. Blog. Available at: http://www.onscenity.org/ (accessed December 10, 2011).

Attwood, F. and C. Smith (2011) Investigating young people's sexual cultures: An introduction. *Sex Education* 11.3, 235–42.

Australian Bureau of Statistics (2007) *Births*. Available at: http://www.ausstats.abs.gov.au/ausstats/subscriber.nsf/0/DC32A0611500BAA0CA2574EF00142139/$File/33010_2007.pdf (accessed October 3, 2011).

Australian Institute of Criminology (2006) *Australian Crime: Facts and Figures*. Canberra: Australian Institute of Criminology.

Australian Institute of Health and Welfare (2007) *Young Australians: Their Health and Wellbeing, 2007*. Canberra: Australian Government. Available at: http://www.aihw.gov.au/publication-detail/?id=10737419261 (accessed February 23, 2011).

Australian Institute of Health and Welfare (2009). *A Picture of Australia's Children*. Canberra: Australian Government. Available at: http://www.aihw.gov.au/publication-detail/?id=6442468252 (accessed February 23, 2011).

Bailey, R. (2011) *Letting Children be Children – Report of an Independent Review of the Commercialisation and Sexualisation of Childhood*. London: Department for Education. Available at: https://www.education.gov.uk/publications/standard/publicationDetail/Page1/CM%208078 (accessed July 6, 2011).

Bajekal, M., V. Osborne, M. Yar and H. Meltzer (2006) *FOCUS ON Health*. London: Office for National Statistics. Available at: http://www.ons.gov.uk/ons/rel/disability-and-health-measurement/focus-on-health/2005-edition/index.html (accessed September 10, 2010).

Bakalar, N. (2012) Teenage Birth Rates Continue to Drop. Available at: http://well.blogs.nytimes.com/2012/04/16/teenage-birth-rates-at-a-low/ (accessed May 1, 2012).

Balliet, T.M. (1928) *Introduction of Sex Education in Public Schools*. New York: American Social Hygiene Association.

Barker, M. and R. Duschinsky (2012) Sexualisation's four faces: sexualisation and gender stereotyping in the *Bailey Review*. *Gender and Education*: Special Issue *Making Sense of the Sexualisation Debates: Schools and Beyond* 24.3, 303–10.

Barnard, I. (2008) *Queer Race: Cultural Interventions in the Racial Politics of Queer Theory*. New York: Peter Lang.

Bauman, Z. (2000) *Liquid Modernity*. Cambridge: Polity.

BBC (2010) Stop sexualising children, says David Cameron. *BBC News*, February 18. Available at: http://news.bbc.co.uk/2/hi/8521403.stm (accessed March 1, 2010).

Benjamin, J. (1998) *Like Subjects, Love Objects: Essays on Recognition and Sexual Difference*. New Haven, CT: Yale University Press.

Berg, B. (2009) *Sexism in America: Alive, Well, and Ruining Our Future*. Chicago, IL: Lawrence Hill Books.

Bernstein, R. (2011) *Racial Innocence: Performing American Childhood from Slavery to Civil Rights*. New York: New York University Press.

Bersamin, M., B. Bourdeau, D. Fisher and J. Grube (2010) Television use, sexual behavior, and relationship status at last oral sex and vaginal intercourse. *Sexuality & Culture* 14.2, 157–68.

Bibring, E. (1943) The concept of repetition compulsion. *Psychoanalytic Quarterly* 12, 486–519.

Biddulph, S. (2008) *Raising Boys: Why Boys are Different – and How to Help Them Become Happy and Well-Balanced Men*. Sydney: Celestial Arts.

Biddulph, S. (2009) How girlhood was trashed and what we can do to get it back: A father's view. In: M.T. Reist (ed.) *Getting Real: Challenging the Sexualization of Girls*. Melbourne: Spinifex Press, 163–70.

Bigelow, M. (1916) *Sex Education: A Series of Lectures Concerning*

Knowledge of Sex in Its Relation to Human Life. New York: Macmillan.

Bollas, C. (2009) *The Evocative Object World*. New York: Routledge.

Bourdieu, P. (1977) *Outline of a Theory of Practice*. Cambridge, MA: Harvard University Press.

Bourdieu, P. (1987) *Distinction: A Social Critique of the Judgement of Taste*. Cambridge, MA: Harvard University Press.

Bourke, J. (2007) *Fear: A Cultural History*. London: Counterpoint Press.

Bragg, S. (2012a) "Blame the moronic mothers": parenting and the sexualization of children debate. Presentation in November, 2012 at: *Pornified? International Conference*, London.

Bragg, S. (2012b) What I heard about sexualization: Or, conversations with my inner Barbie. *Gender and Education* 24.3, 311–16.

Bragg, S., D. Buckingham, R. Russell, R. Willett and N. Dorrer (2012) Children, "sexualization" and consumer culture. *Feminist Media Studies*, forthcoming.

Bray, A. (2008) The question of intolerance: "Corporate paedophilia" and child sexual abuse moral panics. *Australian Feminist Studies* 23.57, 323–42.

Bray, A. (2009) The gaze that dare not speak its name: Bill Henson and child sexual abuse panics. In: M.T. Reist (ed.) *Getting Real: Challenging the Sexualization of Girls*. Melbourne: Spinifex Press, 109–18.

Brottman, M. (2005) *High Theory/Low Culture*. New York: Palgrave Macmillan.

Brown, A. (2002) *Knowledge of Evil: Child Prostitution and Child Sexual Abuse in Twentieth-Century England*. London: Willan.

Brown, A. (2004) Mythologies and panics: Twentieth century constructions of child prostitution. *Children and Society* 18.2, 344–54.

Buckingham, D. (2000) *The Making of Citizens: Young People, News and Politics*. London: University College London Press.

Buckingham, D. (2008) Children and media: A cultural studies approach. In: K. Drotner and S. Livingston (eds.) *The International Handbook of Children, Media and Culture*. London: Sage, 219–36.

Buckingham, D. and S. Bragg (2004) *Young People, Sex and the Media: The Facts of Life?* London: Palgrave Macmillan.

Buckingham, D., R. Willett, S. Bragg, R. Russell and N. Dorrer (2010) External research on sexualised goods aimed at children. Report to Scottish Parliament Equal Opportunities Committee, SP Paper 374. Available at: http://www.scottish.parliament.uk/s3/committees/equal/reports-10/eor10-02.htm (accessed September 1, 2010).

Butler, J. (2004) *Undoing Gender.* New York: Routledge.

Cabrera, Y. (2007) Too sexy too soon? *The Orange County Register,* November 15. Available at: http://www.ocregister.com/news/kil bourne-200398-says-parents.html (accessed May 14, 2008).

Carey, T. (2011) *Where Has My Little Girl Gone?* London: Lion UK.

Celeste Kearney, M. (2006) *Girls Make Media.* New York: Routledge.

Celeste Kearney, M. (2011) Introduction: Girls' Media Studies 2.0. In M. Celeste Kearney (ed.) *Mediated Girlhood: New Explorations of Girls' Media Culture.* New York: Peter Lang, 1–16.

Center for Disease Control (CDC) (2010) Summary health statistics for US children: National health interview survey, 2010. *Vital and Health Statistics* 10.250. Available at: http://www.cdc.gov/nchs/data/series/sr_10/sr10_250.pdf (accessed August 7, 2011).

Center for Disease Control (CDC) (2011) Overweight and obesity statistics in America. Centers for Disease Control and Prevention. Available at: http://www.cdc.gov/obesity/childhood/data.html (accessed August 8, 2011).

Charen, M. (2007) Sexualizing girls: Liberals and conservatives can agree that this is no good at all. *National Review Online.* Available at: http://www.nationalreview.com/articles/220065/sexualizing-girls/mona-charen# (accessed April 2, 2008).

Chodorow, N. (2000) Foreword. In: S. Freud, *Three Essays on the Theory of Sexuality* (trans. J. Stracey). New York: Basic Books, vii–xix.

Cohn, D. (2011). Barely half of US adults are married – a record low. Pew Research Center. Available at: http://www.pewsocialtrends.org/2012/02/16/the-rise-of-intermarriage/ (accessed February 24, 2012).

Coy, M., R. Thiara and L. Kelly (2011) Boys think girls are toys?: An evaluation of the NIA project prevention programme on sexual exploitation. London: London Metropolitan University.

Cross, G. (2004) *The Cute and the Cool: Wondrous Innocence and Modern American Children's Culture.* Oxford: Oxford University Press.

Crowley, M. (2006) No strings attached sex: Teen-girls are buying into the sleaze we're selling. *Reader's Digest Online,* January. Available at: http://www.rd.com/print (accessed May 16, 2008).

Cunningham, H. (2006) *The Invention of Childhood*. London: BBC Books.

Curtis, P. (2011) David Cameron backs proposals tackling sexualization of children. *The Guardian*, June 6. Available at: http://www.guardian. co.uk/society/2011/jun/06/david-cameron-children-sexualization-co mmercialisation (accessed June 15, 2011).

Daily Mail Reporter (2011) The battered and bruised face of Rooney prostitute Helen Wood after she was attacked by drinkers. *Mail Online*, August 10. Available at: http://www.dailymail.co.uk/femail/ article-2024488/Wayne-Rooney-prostitute-Helen-Wood-pictured- battered-bruised-attack.html#ixzz1VCRINS63 (accessed September 11, 2011).

Dalton, P. (2005) Class is out and trash is in. Republished on *Orthodox Canada*. Available at: http://www.orthodoxcanada.org/coment aries/Class%20or%20Trash.htm (accessed November 12, 2011)

Dalven, J. (2012) Use birth control? You're fired! *Ms. Magazine Blog*, March 13. Available at: http://www.msmagazine.com/blog/ blog/2012/03/13/use-birth-control-youre-fired/?fwcc=1&fwcl=1&f wl (accessed March 14, 2012).

Darby, R. (2005) *A Surgical Temptation: The Demonization of the Foreskin and the Rise of Circumcision in Britain*. Chicago, IL: University of Chicago Press.

Davies, B. (2010) Helen's father is an academic, Jennifer's is an oil executive. So what on earth do they think about their girls selling themselves to Wayne Rooney? *Mail Online*, September 9. Available at: http://www.dailymail.co.uk/tvshowbiz/article-1310307/Wayne-Roo ney-scandal-Jennifer-Thompson-Helen-Woods-families-say-sorry.html (accessed August 11, 2011).

de Coninck-Smith, N. (2008) Children's talk and parental fear: Cases of sexual misconduct in Danish state schools 1900–1970. *Journal of Historical Sociology* 21.2, 513–34.

DeMoss, N. (2003) *Becoming a Woman of Discretion: Cultivating a Pure Heart in a Sensual World*. Buchanan, MI: Life Action Ministries.

DeMoss, N. (2011) Interview on Revive our Hearts Radio Show, May 19. Available at: www.reviveourhearts.com/radio/roh/today. php?pid=10870 (accessed June 14, 2011).

DeMoss, N.L. and D. Gresh (2008) *Lies Young Women Believe: And the Truths That Set Them Free*. Chicago, IL: Moody Publishers.

Department for Education (2010) *Youth Cohort Study and Longitudinal Study of Young People in England: The Activities and Experiences of 18 year olds: England 2009*. London: Department for Education. Available at: http://www.education.gov.uk/rsgateway/DB/SBU/b000937/index. shtml (accessed September 20, 2011).

de Visser, R.O., A. Smith, C.E. Rissel, J. Richters and A.E. Grulich (2007) Heterosexual experience and recent heterosexual encounters among a representative sample of adults. *Australian and New Zealand Journal of Public Health* 27.2, 146–54.

Dines, G. (2011) *Pornland: How Porn has Hijacked Our Sexuality*. Boston, MA: Beacon Press.

Dines, G. and J. Long (2011) Moral panic? No. We are resisting the pornification of women: Don't mix up feminists fighting the corporate media with rightwing attempts to police sex. *The Guardian*, January 12. Available at: http://www.guardian.co.uk/comment isfree/2011/dec/01/feminists-pornification-of-women#start-of-com ments (accessed May 12, 2011).

Douglas, M. (2002) *Purity and Danger: An Analysis of Concepts of Pollution and Taboo*. London: Routledge.

Duits, L. and L. van Zoonen (2011) Coming to terms with sexualization. *European Journal of Cultural Studies* 14.5, 1–16.

Durham, M.G. (2008) *The Lolita Effect: The Media Sexualization of Girls and What We Can Do About It*. Woodstock, NY: Overlook Press.

Duschinsky, R. (2010) Feminism, sexualization and social status. *Media International Australia* 135, 94–105.

Duschinsky, R. (2011) Ideal and unsullied: Purity, subjectivity and social power. *Subjectivity* 4, 147–67.

Dworkin, A. (2006) *Intercourse*. New York: Basic Books.

Eating Disorders Victoria (n.d.) Key research and statistics summary. Available at: http://www.eatingdisorders.org.au/key-research-a-statis tics (accessed March 2, 2011).

Edelman, L. (2004) *No Future: Queer Theory and the Death Drive*. Durham, NC: Duke University Press.

Egan, R.D. (2006) *Dancing for Dollars and Paying for Love: Exotic Dancers and their Regular Customers*. New York: Palgrave.

Egan, R.D. (2012) Sexualization and the material girl. *Contexts Magazine* 11.2, 23–5.

Egan, R.D and G. Hawkes (2007) Producing the prurient through the pedagogy of purity: Childhood sexuality and the social purity movement. *Journal of Historical Sociology* 20.4, 443–61.

Egan, R.D. and G. Hawkes (2008) Endangered girls and incendiary objects: Unpacking the discourse on sexualization. *Sexuality and Culture Special Issue on Sexuality, Sexualization and the Contemporary Child* 12, 291–311.

Egan, R.D. and G. Hawkes (2009) The problem with protection: Or, why we need to move towards recognition and the sexual agency of children. *Continuum Journal of Media and Cultural Studies* 23, 389–400.

Egan, R.D. and G. Hawkes (2010) *Theorizing the Sexual Child in Modernity*. London: Palgrave Macmillan.

Egan, R.D. and G. Hawkes (2012) Sexuality, youth and the perils of endangered innocence: how history can help us get past the panic. *Gender and Education: Special Issue Making Sense of the Sexualisation Debates: Schools and Beyond* 24.3, 269–84.

Elias, N. (1996) *The Civilizing Process: Sociogenetic and Psychogenetic Investigations*. Oxford: Blackwell.

Epstein, D., S. O'Flynn and D. Telford (2003) *Silenced Sexualities in Schools and Universities*. London: Trentham Books.

Evans, D.T. (1991) *Sexual Citizenship: The Material Construction of Sexualities*. London: Routledge.

Family Lives (2012) *All of our Concern: Commercialisation, Sexualisation and Hypermasculinity*. London: Family Lives.

Fanon, F. (2008) *Black Skin, White Mask*. New York: Grove Press.

Farley, M. (2009a) Media glamourising of prostitution and other sexually exploitative cultural practices that harm children. In: M.T. Reist (ed.) *Getting Real: Challenging the Sexualization of Girls*. Melbourne: Spinifex Press, 119–30.

Farley, M. (2009b) Prostitution and the sexualization of children. In S. Olfman (ed.) *The Sexualization of Childhood*. Westport, CT: Greenwood, 143–64.

Fass, P. (2006) *Kidnapped: Child Abduction in America*. Oxford: Oxford University Press.

Faulkner, J. (2010) *The Importance of Being Innocent: Why We Worry About Children*. Cambridge: Cambridge University Press.

Ferenczi, S. (1949) Confusions of the tongues between adult and child. *International Journal of Psychoanalysis* 30, 225–30.

Fine, M. (1998) Sexuality, school and adolescent females: The missing discourse of desire. *Harvard Educational Review* 58.1, 29–51.

Fine, M. and S.I. McClelland (2006) Sexuality education and desire: Still missing after all these years. *Harvard Educational Review* 76.3, 297–338.

Finkelhor, D. and L. Jones (2006) Why have child maltreatment and child victimization declined. *Journal of Social Issues* 62.4, 685–716.

Fortenberry, D., V. Schick, D. Herbenick, S. Sanders, B. Dodge and M. Reece (2010) Sexual behavior and condom use at last vaginal intercourse: A national sample of adolescents age 14–17. *International Society for Sexual Medicine* 7.5, 305–14.

Foucault, M. (1980) *History of Sexuality Vol. 1: An Introduction.* New York: Vintage Press.

FPA (2010) Teenage pregnancy factsheet. London: Family Planning Association. Available at: http://www.fpa.org.uk/professionals/fact sheets/teenagepregnancy (accessed September 20, 2011).

Freud, S. (1895) Studies in hysteria (with Joseph Breuer). *Standard Edition* 2, 1–323.

Freud, S. (1900) *Interpretation of Dreams: The Complete and Definitive Text.* New York: Basic Books.

Freud, S. (1905a) *Three Essays on the Theory of Sexuality.* New York: Basic Books.

Freud, S. (1905b) Sexuality in the aetiology of the neuroses. In: P. Reiff (ed.) *Sexuality and the Psychology of Love.* New York: Touchstone Press, 1–10.

Freud, S. (1906) The aetiology of hysteria. *Standard Edition* 3, 191–221.

Freud, S. (1907/1963) The sexual enlightenment of children. In: P. Reiff (ed.) *The Sexual Enlightenment of Children.* New York: Collier Books, 17–24.

Freud, S. (1908a) Civilized sexual morality and modern nervous illness. In: P. Reiff (ed.) *Sexuality and the Psychology of Love.* New York: Touchstone Press, 10–30.

Freud, S. (1908b/2006) On the sexual theories of children. In: *The Psychology of Love* (trans. S. Whiteside). London: Penguin, 221–38.

Freud, S. (1920) Beyond the pleasure principle, *Standard Edition* 18, 3–64.

Freud, S. (1923a) The ego and the id. *Standard Edition* 19, 3–66.

Freud, S. (1923b/1997) The infantile genital organization of the libido: A supplement to the theory of sexuality. In: P. Reiff (ed.) *Sexuality and the Psychology of Love*. New York: Touchstone Press, 161–5.

Freud, S. (1924/1997) The passing of the Oedipus complex. In: P. Reiff (ed.) *Sexuality and the Psychology of Love*. New York: Touchstone Press, 166–72.

Freud, S. (1925) Inhibitions, symptoms and anxiety. *Standard Edition* 20, 157–72.

Freud, S. (1933) *New Introductory Lectures on Psycho-analysis* (trans. J. Strachey). New York: W. W. Norton.

Furedi, F. (2002) *Paranoid Parenting: Why Ignoring the Experts May be Best for Your Child*. Chicago, IL: Chicago Review Press.

Fuss, D. (1995) *Identification Papers: Readings on Psychoanalysis, Sexuality, and Culture*. New York: Routledge.

Fyfe, K. (2008) Skank-o-ween 2008: The sexualization of children. CMI: Culture and Media Institute, October 28. Available at: http://www.mrc.org/cmi/articles/2008/Skankoween__The_Sexualization_of_Children.html%20 (accessed August 1, 2009).

Gallichan, W. (1921) *A Textbook of Sex Education for Parents and Teachers*. Boston, MA: Small, Maynard & Company.

Gans, H. (1999) *Popular Culture and High Culture: An Analysis and Evaluation of Taste*. New York: Basic Books.

Garlick, S. (2010). Taking control of sex? Hegemonic masculinity, technology and internet pornography. *Men and Masculinities* 12.5, 597–614.

Gill, R. (2007) *Gender and the Media*. Cambridge: Polity Press.

Gill, R. (2009) Beyond the "sexualization of culture" thesis: An interactional analysis of "sixpacks", "midriffs" and "hot lesbians" in advertising. *Sexualities* 12.2, 137–60.

Goldman, R. and S. Papson (2011) *Landscapes of Capital*. Cambridge: Polity.

Gonick, M. (2006) Between Girl Power and Reviving Ophelia: Constituting the Neoliberal Girl Subject. *NWSA Journal* 18.2, 1–23.

Gonick, M., E. Renold, J. Ringrose and L. Weems (2009) What comes after girlpower? *Girlhood Studies* 2.2, 1–9.

Good, M.I. (1998) Screen reconstructions: Traumatic memory, conviction and the problem of verification. *Journal of the American Psychoanalytic Association* 46, 149–83.

Gordon, L. (1999) *The Great Arizona Orphan Abduction*. Cambridge, MA: Harvard University Press.

Gorham, D. (1982) *The Victorian Girl and the Feminine Ideal*. Bloomington, IN: Indiana University Press.

Gosine, A. (2008) FOBs, banana boy, and the gay pretenders: Queer youth navigate sex, "race" and nation in Toronto, Canada. In: S. Driver (ed.) *Queer Youth Cultures*. Albany, NY: SUNY Press, 223–43.

Green, H., A. McGinnity, H. Meltzer, T. Ford and R. Goodman (2005) Mental health of young people and children in Great Britain, 2004. London: Office for National Statistics. Available at: http://www.ic.nhs.uk/pubs/mentalhealth04 (accessed September 10, 2011).

Gronow, J. (1997) *The Sociology of Taste*. London: Routledge.

Grossberg, L. (2010) Affect's Future. In: M. Gregg and G.J. Seigworth (eds.) *The Affect Theory Reader*. Durham, NC: Duke University Press, 309–38.

Grossman, L. (2009) It's twilight in America. *Time*, November 13. Available at: http://www.time.com/time/magazine/article/0,91 71,1 938712-1,00.html (accessed June 11, 2011).

Grotstein, J. (1980) The significance of Kleinian contributions to psychoanalysis I: Kleinian instinct theory. *International Journal of Psychoanalytic Psychotherapy*, 8, 375–92.

Guttmacher Institute (2011) Facts on American teens' sexual and reproductive health. Guttmacher Institute. Available at: http://www.guttmacher.org/pubs/FB-ATSRH.html (accessed August 7, 2011).

Haggis, J. (2003) White women and colonialism: towards a non-recuperative history. In R. Lewis and S. Mills (eds.) *Feminist Postcolonial Theory: A Reader*. New York: Routledge, 161–89.

Hala, K. (2009) Twilight arrives in the Arabic world. *The National*, June 26. Available at: http://www.thenational.ae/article/20090626/NATIONAL/706259813 (accessed June 11, 2011).

Hall, L. (2004) Birds, bees and general embarrassment. In R. Aldrich (ed.) *Public or Private Education? Lessons from History*. London: Woburn Press, 98–116.

Hamilton, C. (2007) Brats, bras and tweens. *Insight*. Broadcast April 17, 2007 on SBS Television.

Hamilton, C. (2009) Good is the new bad: Rethinking sexual freedom.

In M.T. Reist (ed.) *Getting Real: Challenging the Sexualization of Girls*. Melbourne: Spinifex Press, 85–98.

Hamilton, M. (2009a) The seduction of girls: The human cost. In: M.T. Reist (ed.) *Getting Real: Challenging the Sexualization of Girls*. Melbourne: Spinifex Press, 55–66.

Hamilton, M. (2009b) *What's Happening to Our Girls? Too Much, Too Soon: How Our Kids are Overstimulated, Oversold and Oversexed*. Sydney: Penguin Group Australia.

Hamilton, M. (2011) *What's Happening to Our Boys? At Risk: How the New Technologies, Drugs and Alcohol, Peer Pressure and Porn Affect Our Boys*. Sydney: Penguin Group Australia.

Haraway, D. (1990) *Simians, Cyborgs and Women: The Reinvention of Nature*. New York: Routledge.

Harris, A. (2003) *Future Girl: Young Women in the Twenty-First Century*. London: Routledge.

Harris, S. (2010) Airbrushed pictures "need warning labels" to prevent insecurity in young girls, government report warns. *The Daily Mail Online*, February 20. Available at: http://www.dailymail. co.uk/news/article-1252361/Government-advisor-Dr-Linda-Papadop oulos-Airbrushed-mags-come-warning-symbols.html#ixzz1fhQ67ZTn (accessed November 2, 2011).

Hatherall, B., N. Stone, R. Ingham and J. McEachran (2005) The chore-ography of condom use: How, not just if, young people use condoms. University of Southampton, The Centre for Sexual Health Research. Available at: http://eprints.soton.ac.uk/40482/ (accessed September 15, 2010).

Hawkes, G. (2004) *Sex and Pleasure in Western History*. Cambridge: Polity Press.

Hawkes, G. and R.D. Egan (2008) Developing the sexual child. *Journal of Historical Sociology: Special Issue on the History of Sexuality of Childhood and Youth* 21.4, 443–65.

Hawkes, G. and R.D. Egan (2012) Complexities and continuities: discourses of childhood sexuality 1830–1940. In: C. Beccalossi and I. Crozier (eds.) *A Cultural History of Sexuality in the Age of Empire (1820–1920)*. Oxford: Berg.

Heins, M. (2001) *Not in Front of the Children: Indecency, Censorship and the Innocence of Youth*. New York: Hill and Wang.

Herbenick, D., M. Reece, V. Schick, S.A. Sanders, B. Dodge and J.D. Fortenberry (2010) Sexual behavior in the United States: Results from a national probability sample of men and women ages 14–94. *The Journal of Sexual Medicine Special Issue: Findings from the National Survey of Sexual Health and Behavior (NSSHB).* Center for Sexual Health Promotion, Indiana University, 255–65.

Hill, A. (2010) After feminism: What are girls supposed to do? Today's teenagers are struggling to cope with the expectations imposed by media images and peer pressure, the reality of low-paid work and a sexist culture. *The Guardian,* February 21. Available at: http://www. guardian.co.uk/society/2010/feb/21/after-feminism-girls-supposed (accessed May 4, 2011).

Hill Collins, P. (2008) *Black Sexual Politics: African Americans, Gender and the New Racism.* New York: Routledge.

hooks, b. (1992) *Black Looks: Race and Representation.* Boston, MA: South End Press.

Huffington Post (2012) Julia Bluhm, 14, leads successful petition for Seventeen Magazine to portray girls truthfully. *Huffington Post,* July 7. Available at: http://www.huffingtonpost.com/2012/07/05/ julia-bluhm-seventeen-mag_n_1650938.html (accessed July 7, 2012).

Hunt, A. (1999) *Governing Morals: A Social History of Moral Regulation.* Cambridge: Cambridge University Press.

Hymowitz, K. (2000) *Ready Or Not: What Happens When We Treat Children As Small Adults.* San Francisco, CA: Encounter Books.

Hymowitz, K. (2002) Thank Barbie for Britney, she's not that innocent. *National Review Online,* May 3. Available at: http://old.nationalreview. com/comment/comment-hymowitz050302.asp (accessed January 3, 2007).

Information Centre for Health and Social Care (2010) Adult trend tables 2009. Health Survey for England – 2009: Trend Tables. Available at: www.ic.nhs.uk/pubs/hse09trends (accessed September 15, 2010).

Irvine, J. (1994) *Sexual Cultures and the Construction of Adolescent Identities.* Philadelphia, PA: Temple University Press.

Irvine, J. (2004) *Talk About Sex: The Battles over Sex Education in the United States.* Berkeley, CA: University of California Press.

Isaacs, S. (1952) The nature and function of phantasy. In: J. Riviere (ed.) *Developments in Psychoanalysis*. New York: Da Capo Press, 67–121.

Jackson, S. (2011) "What's happening to our girls"? Asking different questions about girls and "sexualization." Presentation on December 4, 2011 at: *Pornified? Complicating Debates About the "Sexualization of Culture": An International Conference*. London.

Jackson, S. and S. Scott (2010) *Theorizing Sexuality*. London: Open University Press.

Jackson, S. and T. Vares (2011) Media sluts: Tween girls' negotiations of postfeminist sexual subjectivities in popular media in popular culture. In: R. Gill and C. Scharff (eds.) *New Femininities: Postfeminism, Neoliberalism and Subjectivity*. London: Palgrave, 134–46.

Jackson, S. and E. Westrupp (2010) Sex, postfeminist popular culture and the pre-teen girl. *Sexualities* 13.3, 357–76.

Jacobs, T. (1986) On countertransference enactments. *Journal of the American Psychoanalytic Association* 34.4, 289–307.

James, A., C. Jenks and A. Prout (1998) *Theorizing Childhood*. Cambridge: Polity Press.

Jenkins, P. (2004) *Moral Panic: Changing Concepts of the Child Molester in Modern America*. New Haven, CT: Yale University Press.

Jerselv, A. (2008) Youth films: Transforming genre, performing audiences. In: K. Drotner and S. Livingston (eds.) *The International Handbook of Children, Media and Culture*. London: Sage, 183–95.

Jones, L. and D. Finkelhor (2007) Updated trends in child maltreatment, 2007. Crimes against Children Research Center, University of New Hampshire. Available at: http://www.unh.edu/ccrc/pdf/Updated%20Trends%20in%20Child%20Maltreatment%202007.pdf (accessed April 10, 2011).

Justice Action Australia (2011) Beyond bars: Alternatives to custody. JA: Justice Action. Available at: www.justiceaction.org.au/index.php?option=com_content&task=view&id=165&Itemid=33 (accessed March 5, 2011).

Kaiser Foundation (2003) Virginity and the first time: A series of national surveys with teens about sex. The Henry J. Kaiser Family Foundation and Seventeen Magazine. Available at: http://www.kff.org/mediapartnerships/upload/Virginity-and-The-First-Time-Summary-of-Findings.pdf (accessed March 4, 2011).

Kincaid, J. (1992) *Child Loving: The Erotic Child and Victorian Literature.* New York: Routledge.

Kincaid, J. (1998) *Erotic Innocence: The Culture of Child Molesting.* Durham, NC: Duke University Press.

Kindlon, D. and M. Thompson (2000) *Raising Cain: Protecting the Emotional Life of Boys.* New York: Ballantine Books.

Klein, M. (1937) Love, guilt and reparation. In: M. Klein and J. Riviere, *Love, Hate and Reparation.* London: W.W. Norton, 57–110.

Klein, M. (1946) Notes on some schizoid mechanisms. In: *Envy and Gratitude and Other Works 1946–1963. The Writings of Melanie Klein, Vol III.* New York: Free Press.

Klein, M. (1952) Some theoretical conclusions regarding the emotional life of the infant. In: *Envy and Gratitude and Other Works 1946–1963. The Writings of Melanie Klein, Vol III.* New York: Free Press.

Klein, M. (1959) Our adult world and its roots in infancy. In: *Envy and Gratitude and Other Works 1946–1963. The Writings of Melanie Klein, Vol III.* New York: Free Press.

Klein, R. (2009) The harmful medicalization of sexualized girls. In: M.T. Reist (ed.) *Getting Real: Challenging the Sexualization of Girls.* Melbourne: Spinifex Press, 131–48.

Lafsky, M. (2009) Little girls straight to high heels: How Hollywood continues to oversexualize young women. *New York Post*, November 22. Available at: www.nypost.com/p/news/opinion/opedcolumn ists/little_girls_going_straight_to_heel_7vdPzDvinv7H65elSudcEK#i xzz1LZE91rq0 (accessed November 22, 2009).

Lamb, S. (2001) *The Secret Lives of Girls: What Good Girls Really Do – Sex Play, Aggression, and Their Guilt.* New York: Free Press.

Laqueur, T. (1990) *Making Sex: Body and Gender from the Greeks to Freud.* Cambridge, MA: Harvard University Press.

Lerum, K. and S.L. Dworkin (2009) "Bad girls rule": An interdisciplinary feminist commentary on the report of the APA Task Force on the sexualization of girls. *Journal of Sex Research* 46.4, 250–63.

Levin, D. (2008) Compassion deficit disorder: The impact of consuming culture on children's relationships. In M. Green (ed.) *Attachment and Public Life*, London: Karnac, 122–34.

Levin, D. (2011) Objectified self, objectified relationships: The sexualization of childhood promotes social injustice. In: B.S. Fennimore and L.

Goodwin (eds.) *Promoting Social Justice for Young Children*. New York: Springer Press, 25–34.

Levin, D.E. and J. Kilbourne (2008) *So Sexy So Soon: The New Sexualized Childhood, and What Parents Can Do to Protect Their Kids*. New York: Ballantine Books.

Levine, L. (1990). *Highbrow/Lowbrow: The Emergence of Cultural Hierarchy in America*. Cambridge, MA: Harvard University Press.

Levine, J. (2002) *Harmful to Minors: The Perils of Protecting Children from Sex*. Minneapolis, MN: University of Minnesota Press.

Lewin, T. (2005) Are these parties for real? *New York Times*, June 30. Available at: http://www.nytimes.com/2005/06/30/fashion/thurs daystyles/30rainbow.html?pagewanted=1&_r=1 (accessed January 22, 2011).

Linn, S. (2009) A Royal juggernaut: The Disney princesses and other commercialized threats to creative play and the path to self-realization for young girls. In: S. Olfman (ed.) *The Sexualization of Childhood*. Westport, CT: Praeger, 33–50.

Lipton, M. (2008) Queer readings of popular culture: Searching [to] out the subtext. In: S. Driver (ed.) *Queer Youth Cultures*. Albany, NY: SUNY Press, 163–79.

Lorde, A. (2007) *Sister Outsider: Essays and Speeches by Audre Lorde*. Berkeley, CA: Crossing Feminist Press.

Luker, K. (1985) *Abortion and the Politics of Motherhood*. Berkeley, CA: University of California Press.

Luker, K. (1998) Sex, social hygiene and the state: The double-edged sword of social reform. *Theory, Culture and Society* 27, 601–23.

Lumby, C. and K. Albury (2010) Too much? Too soon? The sexu-alization of children debate in Australia. *Media International Australia, Incorporating Culture and Policy* 135, 141–52.

MacKinnon, C. (1988) *Feminism Unmodified: Discourses on Life and Law*. Cambridge, MA: Harvard University Press.

Mad Dog and Glory (2010) Helen Wood, Jenny Thompson and Wayne Rooney: The Threesome money could certainly buy. *Caughtoffside*, September 9. Available at: http://www.caughtoffside. com/2010/09/09/hooker-pair-helen-wood-jenny-thompson-and-wa yne-rooney-the-threesome-money-could-certainly-buy/ (accessed August 11, 2010).

Magner, M. and G. Hall (2009) Media, marketing creating early sexualization for children, authors find. National Institute on Out-Of-School Time. Available at: http://www.niost.org/pdf/So%20Sexy%20Feb.%202009.pdf (accessed July 5, 2011).

Maines, M. (2009) Something's happening here: Sexual objectification, body image distress, and eating disorders. In: S. Olfman (ed.) *The Sexualization of Childhood*. Westport, CT: Praeger, 63–74.

Males, M. (1996) *The Scapegoat Generation: America's War on Adolescents*. Monroe, ME: Common Courage Press.

Males, M. and D. Macallair (2010) Are teenage criminals getting younger and younger? Exposing another urban legend. The Center on Juvenile and Criminal Justice. Available at: http://www.cjcj.org/files/Are_Tenaage_Criminals_Getting_Younger_and_Younger.pdf (accessed August 7, 2011).

Malik, F. (2005) Mediated consumption and fashionable selves: Tween girls, fashion magazines and shopping. In: C. Mitchell and J. Reid-Walsh (eds.) *Seven Going on Seventeen: Tweenhood Studies in the Culture of Girlhood*. New York: Peter Lang, 257–77.

Marcus, S. (2000). Preface. In: S. Freud, *Three Essays on the Theory of Sexuality*. New York: Basic Books.

Martin, M. (2011) Moms to kids: You can't wear that! Radio Show. *Tell Me More*, April 5. NPR. Transcript available at: http://www.npr.org/2011/04/05/135146130/moms-to-kids-youre-not-going-out-wearing-that (accessed September 4, 2011).

Martinson, F. (1994) *The Sexual Life of Children*. Westpoint, CT: Bergin & Garvey.

McClintock, A. (1995) *Imperial Leather: Race, Gender, and Sexuality in the Colonial Contest*. New York: Routledge.

McInnes, D. (2004) Melancholy and the productive negotiations of power in sissy boy experience. In: M.L. Rasmussen, E. Rolfes and S. Talbert (eds.) *Youth and Sexualities: Pleasure, Subversion and Insubordination in and out of School*. Sydney: Palgrave Macmillan, 223–42.

McInnes, D. and C. Davies (2008) Articulating sissy boy queerness within and against discourses of tolerance and pride. In: S. Driver (ed.) *Queer Youth Cultures*. Albany, NY: SUNY Press, 105–22.

McRobbie, A. (1991) *Feminism and Youth Culture*. London: Macmillan.

McRobbie, A. (2009) *The Aftermath of Feminism: Gender, Culture and Social Change*. London: Sage.

McRobbie, A. and Nava, M (eds.) (1984) *Gender and Generation*. London: Macmillan.

Mental Health Foundation (2000) *All About Anorexia Nervosa*. Mental Health Foundation. Available at: http://www.mentalhealth.org.uk/ (accessed September 20, 2010).

Mercer, C.H., A.J. Copas, P. Sonnenberg, A.M. Johnson, S. McManus, B. Erens and J.A. Cassell (2008) Who has sex with whom? Characteristics of heterosexual partnerships reported in a national probability survey and implications for STI risk. *International Journal of Epidemiology* 38.1, 1–9.

Mindell, J. and K. Sproston (ed.) (2006) Health survey for England 2004: The health of minority ethnic groups. Office for National Statistics. Available at: http://www.ic.nhs.uk/webfiles/publications/hlthsvyeng 2004ethnic/HealthSurveyForEngland161205_PDF%20.pdf (accessed September 14, 2011).

Min Kim, S. (2012) Romney's "get rid of" Planned Parenthood remark becomes Dem fundraising tool. *Politico*, March 14. Available at: http://www.politico.com/blogs/on-congress/2012/03/romneys-get-rid-of-planned-parenthood-remark-becomes-117503.html (accessed March 14, 2012).

Mitchell, C. and J. Reid-Walsh (2005) Theorizing tween culture within girlhood studies. In: C. Mitchell and J. Reid-Walsh (eds.) *Seven Going on Seventeen: Tweenhood Studies in the Culture of Girlhood*. New York: Peter Lang, 1–21.

Mitchell, J. (2000) *Psychoanalysis and Feminism: A Radical Reassessment of Freudian Psychoanalysis*. New York: Basic Books.

Mohanty, C. (2003) *Feminist without Borders: Decolonizing Theory, Practicing Solidarity*. Durham, NC: Duke University Press.

Mooney, B. (2011) What have we come to when middle-class girls like this see whoring as a career choice? *Mail Online*, September 9. Available at: http://www.dailymail.co.uk/femail/article-1310348/ Girls-like-Jennifer-Thompson-Helen-Wood-whoring-career-choice. html?printingPage=true (accessed August 11, 2011).

Mort, F. (2000) *Dangerous Sexualities: Medico-Moral Politics in England Since 1830*. London: Routledge.

Moses, J. (2011) Why do we let them dress like that? Women of a liberated generation wrestle with their eager-to-grow-up-daughters – and their own pasts. *The Wall Street Journal*, March 19. Available at: http://online.wsj.com/article/SB100014240527487038997045762045 80623018562.html (accessed September 4, 2011).

Mulholland, M. (2011) Is there a new normal? Young people negotiate pornification. Presentation on December 4, 2011 at: *Pornified? Complicating Debates about the "Sexualization of Culture": An International Conference.* London.

Nash, J.C. (2008a) Strange bedfellows: Black feminism and anti-pornography feminism. *Social Text* 97, 1–76.

Nash, J.C. (2008b) Re-thinking intersectionality. *Feminist Review* 89, 1–15.

National Institute of Mental Health (2001) *Eating Disorders: Facts about Eating Disorders and the Search for Solutions.* Available at: http://www.nimh.nih.gov/publicat/nedspdisorder.cfm (accessed August 7, 2011).

New England Board of Higher Education (2009) Degrees awarded by gender 1972–2009. Available at: www.nebhe.org/wp-content/up loads/Fig37-2011-cs-degrees-gender-JOH-SA-CC-1.png (accessed August 7, 2011).

OECD (2011) Education at a glance 2011: OECD indicators. Available at: www.oecd.org/document/2/0,3746,en_2649_39263238_48634 114_1_1_1_1,00.html (accessed September 17, 2011).

Olfman, S. (2009) The sexualization of childhood: Growing older younger/Growing younger older. In S. Olfman (ed.) *The Sexualization of Childhood.* Westport, CT: Praeger, 1–6.

Omi, M. and H. Winant (1994) *Racial Formations in the United States.* New York: Routledge.

Oppliger, P. (2008) *Girls Gone Skank: The Sexualization of Girls in American Culture.* Jefferson, NC: McFarland and Company Press.

Orbach, S. (2005) *Hunger Strike: The Anorectic's Struggle as a Metaphor for our Age.* London: Karnac Press.

Paechter, C. (2009) *Being Boys, Being Girls: Learning Masculinities and Femininities.* London: Open University Press.

Palmer, S. (2007) *Toxic Childhood: How the Modern World is Damaging Our Children and What We Can do About It.* London: Orion Press.

Papadopoulos, L. (2010) *Sexualization of Young People Review*. London: Home Office.

Parker, W.H. (1881) *The Science of Life*. Boston, MA: The Peabody Medical Institute.

Pascoe, C.J. (2007) *Dude You're a Fag: Sexuality and Masculinity in High School*. Berkeley, CA: University of California Press.

Peters, C. (2002) G-Strings for seven-year-olds! What's a parent to do? Republished on *NetMuslims*, November 2. Available at: http://forum. netmuslims.com/showthread.php?844-G-Strings-for-Seven-Year-Ol ds!-What-s-a-Parent-to-Do (accessed August 10, 2010).

Pfohl, S. (1992) *Death at the Parasite Cafe: Social Science (Fictions) and the Postmodern*. New York: St. Martin's Press/Macmillan.

Phillips, M. (2010) How did the world's oldest profession become a career choice for middle-class girls? *Mail Online*, September 27. Accessed at: http://www.dailymail.co.uk/femail/article-1315501/ Prostitution-How-did-oldest-profession-career-choice-middle-class-girls.html (accessed August 11, 2011).

Phoenix, A. (2011) Review of recent literature for the Bailey Review of commercialisation and sexualization of childhood. Childhood Research Institute. Available at: http://www.cwrc.ac.uk/projec ts/948.html (accessed June 5, 2011).

Press Association (2003) Girls asked not to wear thong to school. *The Guardian*, May 28. Available at: http://www.guardian.co.uk/educa-tion/2003/may/28/schools.uk2 (accessed December 12, 2006).

Probyn, E. (2010) Writing shame. In: M. Gregg and G.J. Seigworth (eds.) *The Affect Theory Reader*. Durham, NC: Duke University Press, 71–90.

Radorf, L., S. Corral, C. Bradley, H. Fisher, C. Bassett, N. Howat and S. Collishaw (2011). Child abuse and neglect in the UK today. NSPCC. Available at: www.nspcc.org.uk/Inform/research/findings/child_ abuse_neglect_research_PDF_wdf84181.pdf (accessed September 12, 2010).

Raezler, C. (2008) Kids' Halloween costumes get sexy. *Culture and Media Institute*. Available at: http://www.mrc.org/node/28033 (accessed August 10, 2009).

Rand, E. (2003) *Barbie's Queer Accessories*. Durham, NC: Duke University Press.

Rasmussen, M.L. (2004) Safety and subversion: The production of sexualities and genders in school spaces. In: M.L. Rasmussen, E. Rolfes and S. Talbert (eds.) *Youth and Sexualities: Pleasure, Subversion and Insubordination in and out of School*. Sydney: Palgrave Macmillan, 131–52.

Reich, W. (1933/1972) *Character Analysis*, 3rd edn. New York: Simon and Schuster.

Reist, M.T. (2009a) Introduction. In: M.T. Reist (ed.) *Getting Real: Challenging the Sexualization of Girls*. Melbourne: Spinifex Press, 5–40.

Reist, M.T. (ed.) (2009b) *Getting Real: Challenging the Sexualization of Girls*. Melbourne: Spinifex Press.

Reist, M.T. (2011) UK addresses sexualization of children: What's Australia doing? The Drum Opinion of the Australian Broadcast Corporation. Available at: http://www.abc.net.au/unleashed/2750998.html (accessed June 10, 2011).

Renold, E. (2005) *Girls, Boys and Junior Sexualities: Gender and Sexual Relations in the Primary School*. London: Routledge.

Renold, E. and J. Ringrose (2008) Regulation and rupture: Mapping tween and teenage girls' resistance to the heterosexual matrix. *Feminist Theory* 9.3, 313–38.

Renold, E. and J. Ringrose (2011) Schizoid subjectivities?: Re-theorizing teen girls' sexual cultures in an era of "sexualization." *Journal of Sociology* 47.4, 389–409.

Richters, J., A.E. Grulich, R.O. de Visser, A. Smith and C. Rissel (2007) Autoerotic, esoteric, and other sexual practices engaged in by a representative sample of adults. *Australian and New Zealand Journal of Public Health* 27.2, 180–90.

Ringrose, J. (2008) Every time she bends over she pulls up her thong: Teen girls negotiating discourses of competitive heterosexualized aggression. *Girlhood Studies* 1.1, 35–59.

Ringrose, J. (2010) Sluts, whores, fat slags and playboy bunnies: Teen girls' negotiations of "sexy" on social networking sites and at school. In: C. Jackson, E. Paechter and E. Renold (eds.) *Girls and Education: Continuing Concerns and New Agendas*. Maidenhead: Open University Press, 170–82.

Ringrose, J. (2011) Are you sexy, flirty or a slut? Exploring "sexualisation" and how teen girls perform/negotiate digital sexual identity on social networking sites. In R. Gill and C. Sharff (eds.) *New Femininities: Postfeminism, Neoliberalism and Identity*. London: Palgrave, 99–117.

Ringrose, J. (2013) *Postfeminist Education?: Girls and the Sexual Politics of Schooling*. London: Routledge.

Ringrose, J. and E. Renold (2012) Slut-shaming, girl power and "sexualisation": thinking through the politics of the international SlutWalks with teen girls. *Gender and Education*: Special Issue *Making Sense of the Sexualisation Debates: Schools and Beyond* 24.3, 333–43.

Rissel, C.E., J. Richters, A.E. Grulich, R.O. de Visser and A. Smith (2007) First experiences of vaginal intercourse and oral sex among a representative sample of adults. *Australian and New Zealand Journal of Public Health* 27.2, 131–7.

Rivenbark, C. (2006) *Stop Dressing Your Six-Year-Old like a Skank*. New York: St. Martin's Press.

Riviere, J. (1937) Hate, greed and aggression. In: M. Klein and J. Riviere, *Love, Hate and Reparation*. New York, W.W. Norton, 1–56.

Robinson, K. (2008) In the name of innocence: A discursive exploration of the moral panic associated with childhood and sexuality. *Cultural Studies Review* 14.2, 113–29.

Robinson, K. (2012) "Difficult citizenship": The precarious relationships between childhood, sexuality and access to knowledge. *Sexualities* 15.3, 257–76.

Robinson, K. and C. Davies (2008) Docile bodies and heteronormative moral subjects: Constructing the child and sexual knowledge in schooling. *Sexuality and Culture* 12.4, 221–39.

Robinson, M.E. (1911) The sex problem. *Journal of International Ethics* 21, 326–39.

Romesberg, D. (2008) The tightrope of normalcy: Heterosexuality, developmental citizenship, and American adolescence, 1890–1940. *Journal of Historical Sociology* 21.4, 417–42.

Ross, V. (2011) What happened to little girls? *ParentingCanada*. Available at: http://www.parentscanada.com/developing/tweens/articles.aspx?listingid=106 (accessed August 11, 2011).

Rowlands, L. (2011) Kids at school of hard raunch. *Adelaide Now*, May 31. Available at: http://www.adelaidenow.com.au/ipad/kids-at-school-of-hard-raunch/story-fn6t2xlc-1226047337719 (accessed June 11, 2011).

Rubin, G. (1992) Thinking sex: Notes for a radical theory of the politics of sexuality. In C. Vance (ed.) *Pleasure and Danger: Exploring Female Sexuality*. London: Pandora, 267–93.

Rush, E. (2006) Adult world must let girls be girls. *Sydney Morning Herald*, October 10. Available at: http://www.smh.com.au/news/opinion/adult-world-must-let-girls-be-girls/2006/10/09/1160246068431.html (accessed January 3, 2007).

Rush, E. (2009) What are the risks of premature sexualization for children? In: M.T. Reist (ed.) *Getting Real: Challenging the Sexualization of Girls*. Melbourne: Spinifex Press, 41–54.

Rush, E. and A. La Nauze (2006a) *Corporate Paedophilia: Sexualization of Children in Australia*. Australia Institute Working Paper No. 90. Australia Institute, Deakin, ACT. Available at: http://www.tai.org.au/documents/dp_fulltext/DP90.pdf (accessed January 3, 2007).

Rush, E. and A. La Nauze (2006b) *Letting Children be Children: Stopping the Sexualisation of Children in Australia*. Australia Institute Working Paper No. 93. Australia Institute, Deakin, ACT. Available at: http://www.tai.org.au/documents/dp_fulltext/DP93.pdf (accessed January 3, 2007).

Ryan, M. (2010) Why can't I look like that? Asks teenagers. *BBC News*, February 26. Available at: http://news.bbc.co.uk/2/hi/uk_news/education/8537885.stm (accessed August 10, 2011).

Said, E. (1979) *Orientalism*. New York: Vintage Press.

Sammons, M.B. (2011) Tarted up toys. *Circle of Moms*, March 24. Available at: http://www.circleofmoms.com/article/Toys-00165 (accessed August 10, 2011).

Sanchez-Eppler, K. (2005) *Dependent States: The Child's Part in Nineteenth Century American Culture*. Chicago, IL: University of Chicago Press.

Sawyer, M.G., F.M. Arney, P.A. Baghurst, J.J. Clark, B.W. Graetz, R.J. Kosky, B. Nurcombe, G.C. Patton, M.R. Prior, B. Raphael, J. Rey, L.C. Whaites and S.R. Zubrick (2000) Child and Adolescent Component of the National Survey of Health and Well Being. National Mental Health Strategy. Available at: http://www.health.gov.au/internet/main/publishing.nsf/content/70DA14F816CC7A8FCA25728800104564/$File/young.pdf (accessed October 10, 2011).

Sax, L. (2009) *Boys Adrift: The Five Factors Driving the Growing Epidemic of Unmotivated Boys and Underachieving Young Men.* New York: Basic Books.

Schneider, J. (2008) Queer wordplay: Language and laughter in the "boys of boise" morals panic. *Journal of Historical Sociology* 21.4, 466–87.

Shucksmith, J. (2004) A risk worth taking: Sex and selfhood in adolescence. In: E. Burtney and M. Duffy (eds.) *Young People and Sexual Health: Individual, Social and Policy Contexts.* London: Palgrave Macmillan, 5–14.

Siedman, S. (2009) *The Social Construction of Sexuality*, 2nd edn. New York: W.W. Norton.

Smith, C. (2010) Review of: L. Papadopoulos (2010) *Sexualization of Young People Review.* Home Office UK, London. *Participations: Journal of Audience and Reception Studies* 7.1, 175–9.

Stallybrass, P. and A. White (1986) *The Politics and Poetics of Transgression.* Ithaca, NY: Cornell University Press.

Stephens, D. and A. Few (2007) Hip-hop honey or video ho: African American preadolescents' understanding of female sexual scripts in hip-hop culture. *Sexuality and Culture* 11.3, 48–69.

Sternheimer, K. (2003) *It's Not the Media: The Truth about Pop Culture's Influence on Children.* Boulder, CO: Westview Press.

Sternheimer, K. (2006) *Kids These Days: Facts and Fictions about Today's Youth.* New York: Rowman and Littlefield.

Stockton, K.B. (2009) *The Queer Child: Or Growing Up Sideways in the Twentieth Century.* Durham, NC: Duke University Press.

Stoller, A. (1995) *Race and the Education of Desire: Foucault's History of Sexuality and the Colonial Order of Things.* Durham, NC: Duke University Press.

Stoller, A. (2002) *Carnal Knowledge and Imperial Power: Race and the Intimate in Colonial Rule.* Berkeley, CA: University of California Press.

Swain, S. and R. Howe (1995) *Single Mothers and their Children: Disposal, Punishment and Survival in Australia.* Cambridge: Cambridge University Press.

Swain, S., M. Hillel and B. Sweeney (2009) "Being thankful for their birth in a Christian land": Interrogating intersections between whiteness and child rescue. In K. Ellinghaus, J. Carey and L. Boucher (eds.) *Re-Orienting Whiteness.* Sydney: Palgrave Macmillan, 83–98.

Tataro, P. (2006) Silk and lace turn every girl into eye candy. *Sydney Morning Herald*, February 17. Available at: http://www.smh. com.au/news/national/turning-girls-into-eye-candy/2006/02/17/11 40151818732 (accessed July 1, 2008).

Tauber, M., T. Fields-Meyer and K. Smith (2005) Young teens and sex: What's truth, what's just talk and what parents need to worry about: A special report – and People/NBC news poll – on the secret lives of today's teens 16 and under. *People Magazine*, January 31. Available at: http://www.people.com/people/archive/article/0,,20146712,00. html (accessed January 22, 2011).

Taylor, A. (2010) Troubling childhood innocence: Reframing the debate over the media sexualization of children. *Australasian Journal of Early Childhood* 35.1, 48–57.

Thwaites, T. (2007) *Reading Freud: Psychoanalysis as Cultural Theory*. Thousand Oaks, CA: Sage.

Tolman, D. (2005) *Dilemmas of Desire: Teenage Girls Talk about Sexuality*. Cambridge, MA: Harvard University Press.

Travis, A. (2009) Jacqui Smith to tackle "sexualization" culture: Review forms part of three-month national debate on violence against women. *The Guardian*, March 9. Available at: http://www.guard ian.co.uk/society/2009/mar/09/jacqui-smith-sexualization-teenagers\ (accessed April 2, 2009).

Travis, A. (2010) Lads' magazines should be restricted to curb sexu- alization of children report. *The Guardian*, February 25. Available at: http://www.guardian.co.uk/media/2010/feb/25/lads-magazines-re stricted-home-office-study (accessed February 27, 2010).

Tyre, P. (2009) *The Trouble with Boys: A Surprising Report Card on Our Sons, Their Problems at School, and What Parents and Educators Must Do*. New York: Three Rivers Press.

United States Department of Education (2011) Six-year attainment, persistence, transfer, retention, and withdrawal rates of students who began postsecondary education in 2003–04. Institute of Education Sciences: National Center for Education Statistics. Available at: http:// nces.ed.gov/pubs2011/2011152.pdf (accessed August 7, 2011).

Urban Dictionary (2008) Prostitot. Available at: http://www.urbandic tionary.com/define.php?term=prostitot (accessed May 6, 2008).

Vares, T., S. Jackson and R. Gill (2011) Pre-teen girls read "tween" popular culture: Diversity, complexity and contradiction. *International Journal for Media and Cultural Politics* 7.2, 139–54.

Veera, A. (2009) Critique: Report of the APA Task Force on the sexualization of girls. *E-journal Institute for Psychological Therapies* 18.2. Available at: http://ipt-forensics.com/journal/volume18/j18_2.htm (accessed September 30, 2009).

Walker, A., J. Flatley, C. Kershaw and D. Moon (2009) *Crime in England and Wales 2008/09*. London: Home Office Statistical Bulletin. Available at: http://news.bbc.co.uk/2/shared/bsp/hi/pdfs/16_07_09_bcs.pdf (accessed September 20, 2011).

Walkerdine, V. (1991) *School Girl Fictions*. London: Verso Books.

Walkerdine, V. (1998) *Daddy's Girl: Young Girls and Popular Culture*. Cambridge, MA: Harvard University Press.

Walkerdine, V., H. Lucey and J. Melody (2001) *Growing Up Girl: Psycho-Social Explorations of Class and Gender* (Qualitative Studies in Psychology). New York: New York University Press.

Walter, N. (2010) *Living Dolls: The Return of Sexism*. London: Virago Press.

Wang, W. (2012) The rise of intermarriage: Rates, characteristics vary by race and gender. Pew Research Center. Available at: http://www.pewsocialtrends.org/2012/02/16/the-rise-of-intermarriage (accessed February 24, 2012).

Weeks, J. (2009) *Sexualities: Key Ideas*. London: Routledge.

Wellings, K., K. Nanchahal, W. Macdowall, S. McManus, B. Erens, C.H. Mercer, A.M. Johnson, A.J. Copas, C. Korovessis, K.A. Fenton and J. Field (2001) Sexual behaviour in Britain: Early heterosexual experience. *The Lancet* 358.9296, 1843–50.

Welsh Government (2011) *Respecting Others: Sexist, Sexual and Transphobic Bullying*. Guidance Document No. 055/2011.

White, E. (2004) *Fast Girls: Teenage Tribes and the Myth of the Slut*. Berkeley, CA: Berkeley Trade.

Wight, D. and M. Henderson (2004) The diversity of young people's heterosexual behavior. In: E. Burtney and M. Duffy (eds.) *Young People and Sexual Health: Individual, Social and Policy Contexts*. London: Palgrave Macmillan, 15–34.

Willett, R. (2005) Constructing the digital tween: Market discourse and girls' interests. In: C. Mitchell and J. Reid-Walsh (eds.) *Seven Going on*

Seventeen: Tweenhood Studies in the Culture of Girlhood. New York: Peter Lang, 278–93.

Willis, J. (2009) Girls reconstructing gender: Agency, hybridity and transformations of "femininity." *Girlhood Studies* 2.23, 96–118.

Womack, S. (2007) The generation of "damaged" girls. *The Telegraph*, February 20. Available at: www.telegraph.co.uk/health/1543203/The-generation-of-damaged-girls.html (accessed June 10, 2011).

Woods, R. (1999) Too much, too young. *The Times*, September 5. Available at: http://www.fact.on.ca/newpaper/ti99090f.htm (accessed February 28, 2010).

Young, H. and M. Young (2010) *Raising Real Men: Surviving, Teaching and Appreciating Boys*. Smithfield, NC: Great Waters Press.

Zelizer, V. (1985) *Pricing the Priceless Child: The Changing Social Value of Children*. New York: Basic Books.

Zizek, S. (2009) *The Plague of Fantasies*, 2nd edn. New York: Verso.

Index